JourneyThrough®

Psalms 1–50

50 Daily Insights by **Mike Raiter**

Journey Through Psalms 1-50

Our Daily Bread Publishing is affiliated
with Our Daily Bread Ministries.

Requests for permission to quote
from this book should be directed to:
Permissions Department
Our Daily Bread Publishing
P.O. Box 3566
Grand Rapids, MI 49501
Or contact us by email at
permissionsdept@dhp.org

Design by Joshua Tan
Typeset by Grace Goh

ISBN 978-1-913135-20-1

Printed in the United Kingdom
Second Printing in 2020

Foreword

In the church I attend, we read a psalm aloud every Sunday service. This has been the practice of many churches for centuries, and many Christians have made it a habit to read a psalm in their devotions every day.

Reading Psalms is essential for our Christian life and thinking. Theologian John Calvin called Psalms "An Anatomy of All the Parts of the Soul".[1] Whatever experience you are going through, whatever emotion you are feeling, whether the Lord seems near or far away—there is a psalm for you to sing and meditate upon.

Psalms is the most quoted Old Testament book in the New Testament. After His resurrection, Jesus gave His disciples possibly the most important Bible study ever taught. He showed them how "everything must be fulfilled that is written about me in the Law of Moses, the Prophets and the Psalms" (Luke 24:44). Here, the term "Psalms" stands for "writings"—that is, all the Old Testament books of wisdom (Job, Psalms, Proverbs, Ecclesiastes, and Song of Songs).[2] Jesus is teaching His disciples—and us—that all the books of the Bible, including Psalms, speak of Him. In short, in Psalms we see Jesus. Some aspect of the person or work of Jesus is found, prophetically, in almost all the psalms.

As you journey through Psalms, rejoice, weep, and, above all, put your hope in the God who is your Shepherd, Judge, and King.

To God be the Glory,
Mike Raiter

[1] John Calvin, author's preface to *Commentary on the Book of Psalms*, trans. James Anderson (Grand Rapids: Baker, 1998), 1:xxxvii.

[2] Kenneth Barker, ed., *The NIV Study Bible* (Grand Rapids: Zondervan, 1985), 781.

We're glad you've decided to join us on a journey into a deeper relationship with Jesus Christ!

For over 50 years, we have been known for our daily Bible reading notes, *Our Daily Bread*. Many readers enjoy the pithy, inspiring, and relevant articles that point them to God and the wisdom and promises of His unchanging Word.

Building on the foundation of *Our Daily Bread*, we have developed this devotional series to help believers spend time with God in His Word, book by book. We trust this daily meditation on God's Word will draw you into a closer relationship with Him through our Lord and Saviour, Jesus Christ.

How to use this resource

READ: This book is designed to be read alongside God's Word as you journey with Him. It offers explanatory notes to help you understand the Scriptures in fresh ways.

REFLECT: The questions are designed to help you respond to God and His Word, letting Him change you from the inside out.

RECORD: The space provided allows you to keep a diary of your journey as you record your thoughts and jot down your responses.

An Overview

In the Hebrew Bible, the title of the book we call "Psalms" is "Songs of Praise", reflecting its key theme of praising God. The book includes songs from seven named sources: King David, who wrote almost half of the psalms (73 or more);[3] Asaph and the sons of Korah, who probably led worship in the temple (see 1 Chronicles 6:37–39); and Solomon, Moses, Heman, and Ethan.

There are many different kinds of psalms: of thanksgiving (e.g. Psalm 34); of lament (e.g. Psalm 22), which form one third of the psalms; of trust in God's goodness (e.g. Psalm 46); of remembrance of how God saved His people (e.g. Psalm 77); wisdom psalms that contrast two ways of living and the consequences of the choices we make (e.g. Psalms 1, 49); and psalms that foreshadow Israel's king, God's Son and the Anointed One (e.g. Psalm 2). The psalms have not been randomly arranged. There is a careful structure, and often, one psalm continues the theme of the previous one.

Both the songbook of Israel and a Christian book, Psalms opens our eyes to see Jesus, who was promised in these songs, proclaimed in the Gospels, and is present by His Spirit in the lives of His people.

In Colossians, Paul exhorts Christians to "let the message of Christ dwell among you richly as you teach . . . with all wisdom through psalms, hymns, and songs from the Spirit, singing to God with gratitude in your hearts" (3:16). There are two dimensions to our singing: the vertical—singing to God with gratitude—and the horizontal—singing to one another to build each other up. As we study Psalms 1–50, let us both praise God and proclaim His truths to each other.

Key Verse

Serve the LORD with fear . . . Kiss his son, or he will be angry. —Psalm 2:11–12

[3] Tyndale House Publishers, *NLT Study Bible* (Carol Stream: Tyndale House Publishers, 2008), 902.

Day 1

Read Psalm 1

The book of Psalms is like a glorious mansion, built with words of poetry. It is full of many "rooms". There are rooms of praise, thanksgiving, lament, prophecy, and wisdom. The way into this building is through the front doors. Psalms 1 and 2 are the front doors to the book, introducing most of its main themes.

In this first psalm we meet two groups of people who will reappear throughout many of the psalms. The first are the righteous, who love, trust, and obey the Lord. They are blessed by God because they live according to God's direction. They do not walk, stand, or sit like sinners do (Psalm 1:1).

This descending order of actions may be deliberate. Someone begins by walking alongside, then stopping and standing together with, and finally sitting and being a part of the group. This behaviour is what Jesus warned us against when He described His followers as being in the world, but not of the world (John 17:14–15).

God's righteous people delight in God's law (Psalm 1:2). Psalm 1 commends and celebrates meditating on Scripture, which reveals God to us and shows us how to live and please Him. The result is that God's people will be nourished, bear fruit, and prosper (v. 3).

Opposed to the righteous are the second group—the wicked—who rely on themselves and practically despise God's Word and commandments. In contrast to the righteous who are like a fruit-bearing tree (v. 3), the lives of the wicked are like chaff blown away by the wind: dry, fruitless, and withered (v. 4).

The psalm concludes with a final word about these two groups. It reassures the righteous that God cares for them (v. 6). And it warns the wicked, who walk the broad road of disobedience, that their end is destruction (v. 6; see Matthew 7:13).

Psalm 1 is an invitation to take pleasure in reflecting on all of the Word of God. However, most importantly, in the Psalms we will be reminded of the one truly righteous man, the Lord Jesus Christ. Over the next 50 days, He will be our chief meditation and delight.

ThinkThrough

How appropriate is the picture of walking, standing, and sitting for a life of compromise with the world? What practical lessons can you draw from this picture?

What do you find delightful about God's law (Psalm 1:2)?

Day 2

Read Psalm 2

Who is in control in our world? Is it the leaders of the superpowers? Is it the United Nations? No, not according to Psalm 2. The second introduction to Psalms, it puts everything into perspective by reminding us who really controls the world and history.

The psalm begins by portraying the nations working together in conspiracy against God and His anointed one (or "messiah"). The nations want to throw off the shackles of God's authority. It would be terrifying for a tiny nation like Israel to face such a coalition of pagan powers, but God reminds His people that all the plots of the nations are hopeless. The strongest armies are puny next to the power of the Almighty King of heaven. God laughs at their pride and foolishness. He will come in judgment and install His king over all the earth.

Who is this "king" (v. 6) and "anointed" (v. 2)? Who is God's "son" (v. 7) and the heir of all the nations (v. 8)? At the time Psalm 2 was written, this person was David. In 2 Samuel 7:13, God had promised David that his line would rule forever. Sadly, moral and spiritual sin meant that David and his successors could never fulfil God's plans for them. It became clear that all these promises would be fulfilled in a future king. Psalm 2 essentially points forward to the true King and Messiah, the Lord Jesus.

The psalm ends with a warning to all rulers—and, indeed, all people—to fear the Lord and submit to God's son. To "kiss his son" (v. 12) is an act of humble submission (see 1 Samuel 10:1; 1 Kings 19:18). To oppose God's Son will have terrifying consequences ("destruction", Psalm 2:12), but to trust Him will bring great and eternal blessings ("refuge", v. 12).

When God's Son came, the nations raged against Him. The masses and their political and religious authorities opposed Him and put Him to death. Even today, all over the world the nations continue to oppose God and His people. **The message and comfort of Psalm 2 is that one day, before Jesus, every knee will bow and every tongue confess that He is Lord** (cf. Philippians 2:10–11).

ThinkThrough

What does Psalm 2 teach us about God's perspective of the nations? What comfort does this psalm bring to us today?

Make a list of all the things that Psalm 2 teaches us about the Lord Jesus Christ.

Day 3

Read Psalm 3

Knowing God and remaining faithful to Him does not exempt us from trouble and opposition. Sometimes in life these troubles can threaten to overwhelm us. Psalm 3 speaks to this situation.

This psalm reminds us that we should read the psalms on three levels. Firstly, they reflect the life situation of the man who wrote the psalm. Secondly, they point forward to the One who is the subject of all Scripture, the Lord Jesus (see Luke 24:44). Thirdly, they address our own life and experience.

Psalm 2 speaks of those who foolishly try to plot against God's anointed king. Ultimately, their schemes will fail (Psalm 2:1–2). Psalm 3 grounds this truth in history. This is the first psalm which mentions the author and the context of the psalm. David wrote it when he fled from his son, Absalom, who tried to seize the throne (2 Samuel 15–17).

As the psalm opens, we see David almost overwhelmed by the enormity of his opposition. He seems hopelessly outnumbered (Psalm 3:1). Furthermore, enemies mock his faith in God (v. 2).

Yet, this psalm of lament is full of hope. God is David's protective shield and He will restore to him the dignity others want to take away (v. 3). Indeed, so confident is David in the Lord that his troubles don't rob him of a good night's sleep (v. 5).

David asks God to bring judgment on his enemies: "Strike all my enemies on the jaw; break the teeth of the wicked" (v. 7; cf. 2:9). Appropriately, the lament ends with David expressing calm confidence in the God of salvation.

Throughout His life, and especially before the cross, Jesus was surrounded by many who sought to destroy Him, yet He showed godly trust in the face of opposition (Luke 22:42). As the world's true King, He is our supreme example of such faith.

The psalm ends with a blessing on all God's people (Psalm 3:8). Like David, we will sometimes face hostility from others. **At times, the difficult circumstances of life will weigh us down. The God of Psalm 3 is our shield and will lift us up.** Psalm 3 calls us all to look to Him for our deliverance.

ThinkThrough

"Tens of thousands assail me on every side" (Psalm 3:6). Have there been times in your life when you have felt overwhelmed like this? What are some of the things that keep you from trusting in God in such times?

Does God always deliver us from our enemies? What kind of deliverance can we be confident in?

Day 4

Read Psalm 4

It can be hard to keep trusting God when events in life turn against us. We can be tempted to look elsewhere for help and hope. Psalm 4 warns us against putting our confidence in "delusions" and "false gods" (v. 2).

It is difficult to find a precise event in David's life that matches this psalm. However, this gives the psalm a more general character, making it easier for us to apply it to our own circumstances.

Still, we do learn from this psalm that at one point in his reign, King David was distressed. His anguish stems from how his people have turned to idols (v. 2). Later in the psalm, David tells us that the people were longing for prosperity (v. 6); it is possible that this is what led them to foolishly turn to the false pagan gods of fertility. As their divinely appointed leader, David is concerned for their spiritual welfare. The king is honoured when the people obey God, but is shamed by their sin (v. 2). When King David prays, God listens (v. 3); as His anointed king, David rebukes the people for their sinful ways and warns them to repent.

Not all, however, are disobedient. In Psalm 1 we met the righteous who trust in God. Now, David pleads with the people to take a long, hard look at themselves ("search your hearts", 4:4) and follow the godly example of the righteous (v. 5).

If only the people searched their hearts, saw the depth of their sin, and turned back to God, then He would graciously grant them the good things they longed for (vv. 4–6). The people echo the famous blessing of Aaron, "the LORD make his face shine on you and be gracious to you" (Numbers 6:25). God will delight to fill their hearts and lives with joy and abundance, if they "offer the sacrifices of the righteous and trust in the LORD" (Psalm 4:5).

Tough times test our faith. Christians can be tempted to compromise their loyalty to God by turning to delusions like astrology, feng shui, or crystals. Others may put their hope in false gods like money (see Matthew 6:24). This is idolatry. The right response is to "offer the sacrifices of the righteous" (Psalm 4:5), which is a consecrated life of obedience (Romans 12:1–2). As the lives of David and many of God's people testify, in times of trouble this is the true path to joy and peace.

ThinkThrough

There are times in life to "search your hearts and be silent" (Psalm 4:4). What is the purpose and benefit of this self-reflection?

Twice now we've heard David speak of a good night's sleep (3:5; 4:8). According to these psalms, what is the recipe for peaceful sleep?

Day 5

Read Psalm 5

A woman once shared with me that the betrayal of a loved one had made her life hell for years. Few things hurt more, or do more emotional damage, than the unkind or untrue words of others. The book of Psalms reflects, and expresses, how painful this can be. Psalms of lament form the largest category: there are 47 full psalms of lament, while many others contain some lament.

David knew the pain of being a victim of wickedness. In this lament he cries out to God, then waits expectantly for deliverance (Psalm 5:2–3). David is confident God will hear him because He hates evildoers, especially those who hurt others through bloodshed, deceit, and lies (vv. 5–6). You often hear that "God hates the sin but loves the sinner", but it's not that simple. Certainly we confess, "for God so loved the world" (John 3:16), but God does not separate a person from his behaviour. God holds people accountable for their wickedness.

Unlike the wicked, David can enter God's presence. However, he recognises that this privilege comes not from his godly conduct, but out of God's steadfast love, or grace (Psalm 5:7).

David knows the pain of being a victim of enemies whose "throat is an open grave"; lies bring death, not life (v. 9). He calls on God to "declare them guilty" (v. 10). The apostle Paul quotes Psalm 5:9 in Romans 3:13 as he demonstrates that "the whole world [is] accountable to God" (v. 19). But Paul also proceeds to describe how Jesus has atoned for sin so that, by faith, those who were once wicked can be justified and reckoned among the righteous (vv. 21–26).

Like Psalms 3:8 and 4:7–8, Psalm 5 closes with David affirming that the righteous will always be blessed by God and live under His protection (5:11–12). This truth is so wonderful that they will burst out in songs of joy (v. 11).

The woman in my opening story lamented that she was the victim of malice and betrayal. Hurt made her bitter and miserable. She could have trusted God for healing. **Those who love and trust God, like David, may still lament, but they can be confident that God will ultimately hear their prayers, bring justice, and turn their cries for help into songs of joy.**

ThinkThrough

Jesus said, "By your words you will be acquitted, and by your words you will be condemned" (Matthew 12:37). Why does God take so seriously the words that we say?

Psalm 5 is a morning prayer (v. 3). What does this fact teach us about the prayer life of God's people?

Day 6

Read Psalm 6

Many of us are uncomfortable with tears. I'm embarrassed if there are tears in my eyes at the end of a film. Often, we're embarrassed by someone who, while telling us of a struggle or heartbreak in their lives, begins to cry. We might even tell them that there's no need to cry, as if tears are an inappropriate response to suffering. The Bible, however, gives us permission to cry.

In this psalm, David shares that his bed is soaked with tears (Psalm 6:6). When reading the Psalms, we must always bear in mind that this is poetry, and exaggeration is a feature of poems. However, there's still no doubt that David is under great stress in his life.

Whatever the exact circumstances that have led to David's depressed state, he knows that he has no right to demand that God deliver him. As he looks back on the sins in his life, all he can do is to throw himself on God's mercy (vv. 1–2).

Every part of our being is connected. If we're in mental anguish, it can affect our physical, emotional, and spiritual well-being. This is the case with David; his body and his soul are in torment (vv. 2–3).

In such dark times, the first place to turn to is God. Like David, we can trust that He will hear and answer—not because we deserve it, but "because of your unfailing love" (v. 4). Once the Lord has delivered him, David can acknowledge God's goodness in the presence of his people (v. 5).

At the heart of David's sufferings are his enemies (v. 7). We're not given specific details, but they were probably those who sought his life. Enemies take many forms. We may have invisible spiritual enemies seeking to devour us. Sometimes, even life itself can seem to turn against us.

As we drink from the waters of Psalm 6 and reflect deeply on David's words of lament, let us not forget the final wonderful words of hope: the Lord hears his weeping (v. 8) and accepts his prayer (v. 9), and all his—and our—enemies will be overwhelmed (vv. 8–10). And our confidence is even greater than David's because we know that neither "trouble or hardship or persecution or famine or nakedness or danger or sword" can separate us from the love of Christ (Romans 8:35). Along with David, we can be confident that "the Lord has heard my cry for mercy" (Psalm 6:9).

ThinkThrough

What are the things that cause distress in your life?

What are some of the great truths that you can draw from Psalm 6 for comfort in difficult times?

Day 7

Read Psalm 7

It seems that we're all born with an innate sense of justice. One of the first cries of a child who's learnt to speak is: "But that's not fair." Few things make me angrier than injustice, particularly when I think I'm the victim.

The heading of Psalm 7 tells us it's a song which David "sang to the LORD concerning Cush, a Benjaminite". Since the song tells of enemies pursuing David to "tear [him] apart like a lion" (v. 2), it's been suggested that Cush was King Saul's "hit man", sent to find and kill David when Saul grew jealous at his popularity. It was a terrifying prospect for David, who takes refuge in God (v. 1). **A faithful Christian can still trust God while being very scared in frightening circumstances.**

The cry of David's heart is a cry for justice. He's prepared to admit that, if he has done something wrong, even to his enemy (vv. 3–5), then he deserves whatever evil comes to him. But if innocent, he knows the murderous attacks are entirely undeserved.

David's song becomes a prayer. God alone "probes minds and hearts" (v. 9), so He is able to "judge the peoples" (v. 8). David is innocent, so he confidently prays: "Vindicate me, LORD, according to my righteousness, according to my integrity" (v. 8). Let's be clear: David is not claiming to be perfect; he's simply affirming his consistent loyalty both to God and to other people.

The God of justice can be relied upon to save "the upright in heart" (v. 10) as well as to display "his wrath every day" (v. 11) towards the wicked. How will God daily display his wrath? Normally God ordains judgment so that, "whoever digs a hole . . . falls into the pit" (v. 15). The biter will be bitten. Sin has consequences, and a just God will order these consequences.

Let's learn two things from Psalm 7. Firstly, like David, we must keep a clear conscience, knowing that we've not done anything to deserve retribution. Secondly, remember again the Lord Jesus, who, like David, faced enemies who tried to "rip me to pieces" (v. 2). Yet He turned the other cheek and "entrusted himself to him who judges justly" (1 Peter 2:23).

ThinkThrough

When people treat us unjustly, it can make us both hurt and angry. What can we learn from Psalm 7 and the experience of the Lord Jesus in how to respond to injustice?

David writes that God "displays his wrath" every day (v. 11). Paul says the same thing in Romans 1:18–27. What evidence do King David and the apostle Paul see of God's wrath operating in the world?

Day 8

Read Psalm 8

Romans 3:23 says: "For all have sinned and fall short of the glory of God". This is true and we must never forget that we are all sinners. But that's not the whole story. We may have fallen short of God's glory, but we've not lost it altogether.

The human being is a paradox: capable of horrendous evil but also of wonderful acts of kindness. We ruin and destroy God's earth, while also displaying breathtaking beauty and creativity. Psalm 8 extols both the supreme glory of God and the wonder of the human being who is the pinnacle of His creation.

First, however, it begins by reminding us of the majesty of the Creator God (v. 1). Even the sum total of human achievement is dwarfed by the One who set the moon and stars in their place. According to science magazine *Scientific American*, our Milky Way alone contains over one trillion planets. And that's just one galaxy in a universe of at least 100 billion —all the work of God's hands.

How amazing, then, that this God should care for us. And, more than that, as David says of humanity, God has "made them [only] a little lower than the angels" (v. 5). David is thinking of Genesis 1, which tells us that we're made in God's image. We are not like the animals. Unique to all creation, humans are "crowned . . . with glory and honour" (Psalm 8:5).

Furthermore, we have been appointed to be caretakers of God's world (vv. 6–8, see Genesis 1:28–29). In 1 Corinthians 15:27, Paul quotes Psalm 8:6, but applies it to Jesus. Referring to the resurrection, Paul says that God has put everything under the feet of Jesus. He is the true human being because Psalm 8 is truly fulfilled in Him alone. Only Jesus could control winds and waves and heal diseases, because only He had full dominion over everything. Our great hope as Christians is that one day we'll be like Jesus, and will fully reflect Psalm 8.

Today, let's thank God for those signs of humanity's glory and dignity, but let us also remember the note on which this psalm begins and ends (vv. 1, 9). If a Taj Mahal or a Versailles are monuments to human creativity, then stand in awe at Niagara Falls or the Himalayas. If the intricacies of computers impress you, stand amazed at the human brain which God designed. So, then, "Lord, our Lord, how majestic is your name in all the earth!" (v. 1).

ThinkThrough

What can you thank God for in your fellow human beings? What evidence do you see of our glory and honour?

Reflecting on the life and ministry of the Lord Jesus, how can we see Him perfectly fulfilling what is written in Psalm 8?

Day 9

Read Psalm 9

How many of us have faced real enemies? Certainly, there are people whom we don't get along with or who may not like us very much. But most of us meet very few people who set out to do us great harm. David, on the other hand, faced much deadlier opposition.

As the king of a tiny nation, David was acutely aware that he was surrounded by warlike, hostile, and unbelieving enemies. An important part of a king's job was to protect and defend his people by leading his army into battle. Having previously asked for God's deliverance, David now gives thanks for the divine protection he has received (Psalm 9:2).

By God's grace and power, Israel had known success and prosperity for much of David's reign. The Lord had given them victory over their enemies. He had demonstrated His righteous nature by blotting the wicked out of existence (v. 5), fulfilling the promises He had made to Israel's forefathers (see Genesis 12:3).

God's church is not a political nation, and our king, the Lord Jesus, reigns from heaven over a spiritual kingdom. But we can learn three things from this psalm.

Firstly, as Christians we know that ultimately our enemies aren't flesh and blood, but spiritual powers and authorities (Ephesians 6:12). In Psalm 9:5, David speaks of his enemies as if they have been finally and completely vanquished: "You have blotted out their name for ever and ever." Of course, Israel's enemies would continue to oppress her. Similarly, we know that these dark spiritual forces were defeated by Jesus' death on the cross, but they still oppress us and try to make us lose heart. Yet, we have the same comfort as David, that the Lord is "a stronghold in times of trouble" (v. 9), and that He will ultimately deliver us.

Secondly, David variously describes "those who know your name" (v. 10) as "the oppressed" (v. 9), "those who seek you" (v. 10), "the afflicted" (vv. 12, 18), and "the needy" (v. 18). All these terms express our spiritual weakness and our utter dependence on God. **We must always remember our essential helplessness, so that we daily turn to the God who "reigns for ever" (v. 7) and who will never forsake us or forget us.**

Finally, Psalm 9 reminds us that God "rules the world in righteousness and judges the peoples with equity" (v. 8). While this judgment is sometimes experienced here and now (vv. 15–16), the final end of all

God's enemies is certain. The great hope of the righteous is that they "will never perish" (v. 18). These great truths encouraged David to be "glad and rejoice" (v. 2), and they made the heavenly multitude sing hallelujah (Revelation 19:1–3).

ThinkThrough

Read through Psalm 9 again and write down what it tells us about the character and works of our God.

Again and again David calls on God's people to tell of His wonderful works (vv. 1, 11, 14). How, where, and what should we be proclaiming to the nations?

Day 10

Read Psalm 10

Psalm 9 is David's personal testimony. It speaks briefly of the persecution he faces (v. 13), but David is chiefly thankful that evildoers will face judgment because "the Lord is known by his acts of justice" (v. 16). The theme of the oppression of the innocent continues in Psalm 10, but here, David (presumably the author of this psalm) applies what he has just said not only to his own situation, but also to all who are needy and oppressed as a result of the sinfulness of the wicked.

That's why it's important to read Psalms 9 and 10 together. Indeed, in the Greek translation of the Hebrew Old Testament (called the Septuagint), Psalms 9 and 10 are considered one psalm. Furthermore, there's no heading ("For the director of music . . .") before Psalm 10, suggesting that it belongs with Psalm 9.

Psalm 10 describes the character and deeds of the wicked person. It describes his brutal and exploitative treatment of "the weak" (v. 2). The oppressed are sometimes caught in his evil schemes, crushed, and even murdered. We saw in Psalm 1, the introduction to the Psalter, that "the wicked" stand in opposition to "the righteous". Not only do the wicked revile the Lord (10:3), but they also persistently oppress God's people, who are innocent, helpless, and oppressed (vv. 8, 12, 18).

The abusive conduct of the wicked is rooted in his contempt for God and His laws. In particular, he has convinced himself that he has no need to fear the coming judgment. "He says to himself, 'God will never notice'" (v. 11). **When we stop believing in the all-seeing eyes of God, we are easily tempted to indulge in all sorts of evil behaviour.**

The apostle Paul quotes Psalm 10:7 in Romans 3:14 as part of his evidence that "all have sinned" (Romans 3:23). Psalm 10 isn't simply God's description of a handful of "really bad" people, but a diagnosis of the character of the human race.

The problem for the believer is that God sometimes seems to sit back and do nothing while the wicked are on the rampage (Psalm 10:1). David, however, ends his bleak but brutally honest portrayal of the wicked by reminding us to pray, calling on God to not forget the helpless (v. 12), and to continue trusting in Him, because ultimately the Lord will hear and defend His people (vv. 17–18).

ThinkThrough

If someone were to ask you the question that David poses, "Why does God hide himself in times of trouble?", from what we have read in Psalms 9 and 10, what answer could you give?

David describes the Lord as "the helper of the fatherless" (Psalm 10:14). Why is this such an appropriate metaphor for God's suffering people?

Day 11

Read Psalm 11

If your life is in danger because of your faithfulness to God, when do you stay and when do you go? When the apostle Paul faced danger, he sometimes fled (e.g. Acts 17:10); at other times he chose to stay and face the suffering (e.g. Acts 21:10–14). Deciding when to stay and when to flee requires wisdom. For the apostle Paul, it was often a matter of discerning which course of action was more strategic for the spread of the gospel. For David, it was a question of expressing his confidence in the power and protection of God.

In Psalm 10, David described the contempt that the wicked have for God, and then expressed his confidence that the Lord would protect him from the attacks of such people. Now, in Psalm 11, David tells us again why he has such faith in God.

The psalm begins with David rejecting advice to run away from an enemy. We don't know the particular event, except that once again David's life is in danger. He's told to run and hide because the situation is helpless (Psalm 11:1). David is even warned that once such enemies set out to harm you, "what can the righteous do?" (v. 3). Of course, there were times when wisdom dictated that David should run away (e.g. 1 Samuel 20, 2 Samuel 15), but not because he'd lost faith in God's power and love. In this case, however, the advice David's been given simply expresses no faith in the sovereign God, and he is right to reject it.

In the second half of the psalm, David sings of God's power to protect His people. Since God sits on a heavenly throne (Psalm 11:4), He observes everything that happens. People may think that David is in mortal danger, but the reality is that his enemies—who are also God's enemies—are in even greater danger. It is terrifying to face the wrath of God (v. 6).

David observes that God hates the wicked with a passion (v. 5). But, you might wonder, doesn't God love everyone? Yes, He does, and His arms are always open, inviting sinners to turn to Him (see 4:4–5). But those who persist in evil remain under His terrifying wrath (11:5–6).

Let's be encouraged today that the Lord's watchful eyes are upon us, and that He will bring justice at the right time.

ThinkThrough

How can we discern when might be the right time to flee suffering and persecution, and when to stay and face it?

Read John 15:18: "If the world hates you, keep in mind that it hated me first." Why does Jesus draw such a close connection between how people treat His disciples and how they treat Him? How should we respond to this truth?

Day 12

Read Psalm 12

Emily Dickinson, a famous American poet, once wrote a short but profound poem:

A word is dead when it is said, some say. I say it just begins to live that day.[4]

Once a word is spoken, we cannot take it back. And words are very powerful: they can heal or destroy, and they can bring life or death.

Psalm 12 explores the significance of words. At the beginning of the psalm David is deeply discouraged because he looks around him and sees so few people who are loyal to the Lord: "No one is faithful any more" (v. 1). The evidence for this is found in their speech. Listening to the ungodly, he hears lies, flattery, deception, and boasting (vv. 2–3). They think they're free to say whatever they want, and no one will hold them to account (v. 4).

Words of truth are the bedrock of relationships.

When our speech is marked by lies and deception, there can be no trust, friendship, or real communication; families, churches, and society as a whole break down.

The righteous and the poor and needy are the victims of the tongues of the wicked. Once again, David turns to God and rejoices in His words, because He promises to rescue His people "from those who malign them" (v. 5). David, who is God's faithful servant, identifies himself with these oppressed people, saying that God "will protect *us* for ever from the wicked" (v. 7, emphasis added). Unlike the words of the wicked, God's words can be trusted because they are "flawless", like purified silver and gold (v. 6).

It is often said that the eyes are the mirror of the soul. But that's not true. If you want a window into someone's soul, listen to his speech. Jesus said, "the mouth speaks what the heart is full of", and that's why we will be condemned or acquitted by our words (Matthew 12:34, 37).

Paul encourages us not to let unwholesome speech come out of our mouths, but only what builds up (Ephesians 4:29). To be part of a community where conversations are filled with words of truth, kindness, encouragement, humility, and praise would be, as David the songwriter knows, something worth singing about.

[4] Emily Dickinson, BrainyQuote.com, 10 December 2018, https://www.brainyquote.com/quotes/emily_dickinson_126002.

ThinkThrough

Why does David liken the words of God to purified silver and gold? What is it about these metals that make them such an effective illustration of God's speech?

What can we do as individuals and as a church to ensure that we build up one another by our speech?

Day 13

Read Psalm 13

Many Christians will admit that they find it hard to pray. Amid life's busyness, it's difficult to maintain a regular, disciplined prayer life. In particular, it can be hard to keep on praying when God doesn't seem to hear or answer. We pray to find a job. We pray for healing. We pray for the salvation of family members. But it sometimes seems that these prayers are falling on God's deaf ears.

Many of the psalms express this kind of frustration, with God's faithful people wondering why God seems so distant in their time of suffering. In the opening two verses of Psalm 13, David asks the Lord four times: "How long?" David feels forgotten by the Lord, and wonders if God will ever listen to his cries for help (v. 1). Once again, the cause of his sorrow is some unnamed enemy. But God's silence has made his anguish even deeper, so there is sorrow in his heart (v. 2).

At the beginning of the psalm, David prays: "How long will you hide your face from me?" (v. 1). Then he prays for the Lord to turn around and "look on me" (v. 3). Back in Numbers, God told Aaron to say to Israel: "The LORD bless you and keep you; the LORD make his face shine on you and be gracious to you; the LORD turn his face towards you and give you peace" (Numbers 6:24–26). God turns His face towards us to bless us, and this is what David asks of the Lord.

Psalms is full of songs like these, where God's people lament. In almost every case, though, the final words are not of despair, but hope. Here, David trusts and rejoices in God's salvation and sings of God's goodness. This doesn't mean that he's stopped hurting and his problems have disappeared, but in the midst of lament he can have faith and rejoice.

God gives us permission to express our human emotion and cry out: "How long, Lord?" The Lord knows that maintaining faith while living in a hostile world isn't easy, and He has given us songs of sorrow to pour out our troubles to Him and to reassure ourselves of His faithfulness and power.

We usually don't know why the Lord sometimes seems to delay in answering prayer. In a parable about a persistent widow (Luke 18:1–8), Jesus tells us that He will definitely hear and answer our cries for justice. In the meantime, let us remain faithful in prayer, for "when the Son of Man comes, will he find faith on the earth?" (v. 8).

ThinkThrough

Have you had prayer experiences in which God seemed to be a long time in answering? How should we respond in such situations?

In the midst of hurts, doubts, and sorrows, how can David still sing praises to God? What can we learn from this?

Day 14

Read Psalm 14

Jesus once told a story about a rich farmer whom God blessed with abundant harvests. He kept storing his surplus crops so that he could relax and indulge himself. Jesus concluded: "But God said to him, 'You fool! This very night your life will be demanded from you'" (Luke 12:20). This man was foolish because he didn't fear God and the coming judgment, and didn't use his wealth to care for those in need (see v. 33).

We meet the same kind of fool in Psalm 14. In the Bible, folly is both intellectual and practical. It's expressed in how we think and how we live. David goes on to describe such people as "corrupt, their deeds are vile" (v. 1). As in many of his other psalms, he is describing the wicked in Israel who oppress God's people. "They devour *my people* as though eating bread . . . evildoers frustrate the plans of the poor, but the LORD is their refuge" (vv. 4, 6, emphasis added).

You see, folly of the heart is often expressed by wickedness in action. The fool says: "There is no God" (v. 1). This doesn't mean the fool is an atheist. He believes in God, but lives as if He weren't there.

Sadly, there are people in the church who are like this. They may recite a creed and sing songs of praise, but in their everyday life they are practical atheists. The fact that God "looks down from heaven" (v. 2) and will judge them one day never enters their thinking and, therefore, never affects how they live.

There is, however, a group of people who have called upon the Lord and look to Him for refuge. He is "present in [their] company" (v. 5) and will deliver them one day. The psalm ends with David looking forward to that day when there'll be "salvation for Israel" from Zion (v. 7). David never lived to see that day, but we have. And David could never have imagined how God would bring salvation to the entire world through His own descendant, the Lord Jesus.

Paul quotes Psalm 14:1–3 in Romans 3:11–12 to demonstrate that "all have turned away". He then reminds us that God has brought salvation through the atoning death of Jesus. By this salvation—even greater than the one David had hoped for—the Lord has destroyed all our enemies and given His people an eternal restoration and inexpressible joy (Psalm 14:7).

ThinkThrough

Paul says this of humanity: "Although they claimed to be wise, they became fools" (Romans 1:22). What evidence of this foolishness does he give (vv. 23–32)? What similarities can you see between this passage and Psalm 14?

"There is no one who does good, not even one" (Psalm 14:3). Of course, we all know good people who aren't Christians, and bad people who are capable of some good deeds. What do you think, then, that David (and Paul in Romans 3) means by this?

Day 15

Read Psalm 15

If someone today wants to know how to be saved, they might ask us: "What do I need to do to get to heaven?" Or: "How can I find eternal life?" We would then tell them the good news about what Jesus has done to win our salvation. In the Old Testament, such questions were asked a bit differently.

The Israelites believed that, symbolically, God lived among them in His temple in Jerusalem, the city on a hill. To ascend the mountain of the Lord was to enter God's presence. In Psalm 15, David is really asking: "Who can live forever in your presence?" Perhaps the answer David gives surprises us. But it shouldn't.

Israel was God's chosen people, rescued from slavery in Egypt and set free to be His holy nation. As long as they lived lives of holiness, they would remain in the land God had given them and live in His presence (Deuteronomy 11:8–9). The Bible regularly uses "walking" to describe living a life that is pleasing to God (see Psalm 1:1). David describes the relationships we are to have as we walk with one another: we speak the truth to each other and do good to our neighbours (15:3), keep our promises (v. 4), and don't exploit the poor (v. 5).

It sounds like the righteous person here is perfect ("who does no wrong", v. 3), but it's the Bible's way of speaking about the consistency of a person's life. This is biblical faith.

In the Sermon on the Mount, Jesus gives a fuller exposition of what David sings about here. Jesus teaches about the importance of keeping our oaths (Matthew 5:33–37), doing good (7:12), and caring for the poor (6:3). These are the marks of those who've experienced God's salvation and live under His rule. **A life of love to others is the required response to the God of love who's been gracious to us.** "Whoever does these things will never be shaken" (Psalm 15:5).

ThinkThrough

In Titus 1:6–9, Paul describes the qualifications for being an elder. As with Psalm 15:2, the first thing he mentions is "blameless" (Titus 1:6). What does it mean to be blameless, and why is this kind of life so important to God?

In what ways should our treatment of others reflect how God treats us?

Day 16

Read Psalm 16

The longing to be happy is one of the most basic of all human desires. For example, parents will often pay a lot of money to ensure their children receive a good education, because they see it as the pathway to finding a satisfying, well-paid job—and therefore happiness. Happiness is a God-given desire. He wants us to be happy now, and to have an even happier eternity. Our problem is not in craving happiness, but in where we think we'll find it.

Psalm 16 is a wonderfully joyful song. David begins by rejoicing that God is his refuge (v. 1). Then he sings, "apart from you I have no good thing" (v. 2). Later he describes God as "my portion and my cup" (v. 5), his food and drink. In other words, David is rejoicing in the fact that God is all that he needs.

David also takes delight in "the noble ones" (v. 3). The Lord rejoices in us when we stay faithful to Him.

One reason David delights in the Lord is that "the boundary lines have fallen for me in pleasant places" (v. 6). When the tribes of Israel settled in the Promised Land, each tribe was assigned pieces of land. So, David says, I've been blessed because I've been given a pleasant piece of land. But remember, this is poetry. He's talking not just about geography, but about all the blessings God has poured on him.

Finally, David is full of joy because there are "eternal pleasures at your right hand" (v. 11). **Many people make the mistake of tying happiness to earthly things like possessions or experiences. But the greatest joy is knowing God, and we have the wonderful prospect of living with Him forever** (v. 11).

When Peter was preaching at Pentecost, he quoted Psalm 16:8–11 in saying that God did not abandon Jesus to the grave (Acts 2:26–28). This is a wonderful comfort to us who follow Him. God will never abandon us too, even in death; instead, He will bring us into eternal joy. Peter's sermon helps us understand that, pre-eminently, David's song was pointing to Jesus, whom God raised from the dead. Because God did not abandon Him to the realm of the dead, even now Jesus is filled with joy in the Father's presence.

ThinkThrough

It's good to find joy in the things of earth. When, and how, can these things replace the joy we should find in knowing God?

"I keep my eyes always on the LORD" (Psalm 16:8). What practical steps can we take to daily keep our focus on the Lord?

Day 17

Read Psalm 17

We can't be sure when David wrote this psalm, but the events recorded in 1 Samuel 24 would fit very well. Saul, who was trying to hunt down and kill David, had unwittingly entered a cave where David and his men were hiding. David's men thought this was a God-given opportunity to kill the corrupt king. but David knew that Saul, for all his faults, was God's anointed king, so he couldn't lay a hand on him. Letting him go, David called out to Saul: "I have not wronged you, but you are hunting me down to take my life" (1 Samuel 24:11). He assured Saul that he would never harm him; rather, "may the LORD avenge the wrongs you have done to me" (v. 12).

David prayed for God's deliverance from his enemy. If, while praying that prayer, he'd been planning his own vengeance, then the prayer would have been deceitful (Psalm 17:1). David knows that there is something more valuable than his life, and that is his personal integrity. God knows all about David; as David sings, "you examine me at night and test me" (v. 3). This is just as true for us and so, like David, we should ensure that the words of our lips and the meditations of our heart (Psalm 19:14) are one.

In the midst of this psalm, David paints two lovely pictures of his relationship with his God. He asks the Lord: "Keep me as the apple of your eye" (Psalm 17:8). The eye is the most cherished part of the body; on a number of occasions, the Lord uses this tender expression to describe His affection for His people (see Deuteronomy 32:10; Zechariah 2:8). Here, it expresses the very special place David has in God's heart.

David then goes on to say: "Hide me in the shadow of your wings" (Psalm 17:8). David frequently used this image of the mighty eagle, whose little ones find safety under its majestic wings (see Psalms 36:7; 57:1; 61:4; 63:7).

No one is a greater object of God's delight than His own Son, the Lord Jesus. He is the eternal apple of the Father's eye. **There is wonderful comfort in knowing that we who love the Son and are His brothers and sisters by adoption, share in the Father's delight.** There is no greater privilege than to be the apple of God's eye.

ThinkThrough

What is the basis for David's confidence that God will hear and answer his prayers (Psalm 17:1)? How should that influence our prayer requests?

"Show me the wonders of your great love" (v. 7). How has the Lord shown you the wonders of His love?

Day 18

Read Psalm 18

I recently attended the funeral of a man who was a regular churchgoer. In all the eulogies recounting his life, there was no mention of God or faith. David probably composed Psalm 18 near the end of his life. Looking back, he remembers "when the LORD delivered him from the hand of all his enemies and from the hand of Saul" (2 Samuel 22:1). This song is the story of David's life, and speaks of God and His faithfulness.

There are three parts to Psalm 18. In verses 1 to 19, David praises God because He is his deliverer. David knew where to turn when in danger or difficulty: "I called to the LORD" (vv. 3, 6). At times in his life, he could feel the breath of approaching death; it was like being swept away by a raging river and dragged underwater (vv. 4–5). In the most dramatic imagery that reminds us of Israel's deliverance from Egypt, David describes how God came and saved him (vv. 6–17). David is rescued from his enemies by the same power that parted the Red Sea.

Similarly, Paul tells Christians of God's "incomparably great power for us who believe. That power is the same as the mighty strength he exerted when he raised Christ from the dead" (Ephesians 1:19–20).

In Psalm 18:20–27, David acknowledges that God has dealt with him "according to my righteousness" (v. 20). We may wonder how an adulterer and murderer like David (see 2 Samuel 11) can make such a claim. David was deeply aware of his sins and God's forgiveness (see Psalm 51), but he also knew that the Lord looks for a life of consistent obedience from those who trust Him. Looking back on his life, he can affirm that he's been faithful to the Lord (Psalm 18:21–23). **We who regularly seek God's forgiveness also take seriously Jesus' words that it is the pure in heart who will see God** (Matthew 5:8).

Finally, David acknowledges that all he has accomplished was by the supernatural power of God (Psalm 18:28–50). Speaking of his enemies, he can sing: "I crushed them so that they could not rise" (v. 38); and: "You made my enemies turn their backs in flight" (v. 40). The apostle Paul had the same confidence, exhorting us to "continue to work out your salvation . . . for it is God who works in you" (Philippians 2:12–13).

ThinkThrough

At this point in your life, whether young or old, how would you testify of God's enduring faithfulness to you?

How do we reconcile the reality of our sufferings with the victorious sentiments that David expresses in Psalm 18:28–50? Compare David's words in this time of trial with Paul's words in 2 Corinthians 4:7–18.

Day 19

Read Psalm 19

Christian writer C. S. Lewis once said about Psalm 19: "I take this to be the greatest poem in the Psalter and one of the greatest lyrics in the world."[5] It's a symphony of praise to God's Word in three movements.

First, we hear the silent voice of God (vv. 1–6). The heavens declare, proclaim, and pour forth divine knowledge. So, when David says, "they have no speech, they use no words; no sound is heard from them" (v. 3), he is saying that while creation's voice is inaudible to the human ear, its message can be clearly heard: God still speaks through it. That's why, says Paul, men and women have no excuse for not giving Him the glory (Romans 1:18–20). **The danger for us is that we, too, can be deaf to the glorious music of creation that the Lord plays for us every day.**

Second, David rejoices at the voice of God in His Word (Psalm 19:7–10). Of course, both voices—creation and Scripture—sing the same song: the glory of God. Where creation reveals God's glory, Scripture follows by providing greater detail. While David is focusing on the Law of Moses (v. 7), what he says is true of all Scripture. David describes the Bible's life-changing impact: it refreshes the soul, makes us wise, gladdens the heart, and gives light to the eyes (vv. 7–8). No wonder David sings that the Word is worth more than the world's gold, and tastier than the most delicious food (v. 10).

Finally, David responds to the God who speaks (vv. 11–14). He describes one feature of the Word's ministry in the life of the righteous: the conviction of sin. David asks God for forgiveness for both his hidden faults and his deliberate sins (vv. 12–13). God's Word announces our sinfulness and speaks of our need for cleansing. But the wonderful climax of its message is that God's Word became flesh and dwelt among us (John 1:14). This living Word made us clean by His death and rules us by His gospel. By His Word and Spirit, God changes lives, and by reading and obeying all of God's word, "there is great reward" (Psalm 19:11), even into eternity.

[5] C. S. Lewis, Reflections on the Psalms (New York: Harper One, 1958), 73–74, https://reiterations.wordpress.com/2017/07/26/c-s-lewis-on-psalm-19/.

ThinkThrough

How much thought do you give to the "symphony of creation"? What does creation teach us about the God we worship? What can we do to create a greater awareness of the voice of God in creation?

How has reading God's Word affected your life?

Day 20

Read Psalm 20

The New Testament encourages us to pray for those in authority over us, so that we might live peaceful and quiet lives (1 Timothy 2:2). The Bible recognises that the welfare of a nation is tied to the effectiveness of those in government. A nation will struggle to progress under weak or corrupt rulers, while just and competent governments bring peace and prosperity.

Psalm 20 explores the relationship between the king, who is the Lord's anointed, and his people. The psalm opens with the people praying for the safety and success of their king (vv. 1–4), who appears to be about to go out into battle (v. 5). They are praying for him because the victory of the king is their victory. When the Lord hears their prayers and makes all the king's plans succeed (v. 4), then the whole nation will rejoice, because they, too, will "rise up and stand firm" (v. 8).

Verse 6 is likely the king responding to the prayers of his people. He is confident that God will grant success to His anointed. Back in Psalm 2 we first met the Lord's anointed, or messiah. God had appointed him ruler over his people, and guaranteed him victory over his enemies (Psalm 20:6–8). We saw that while these words were written about King David, their true fulfilment was in his descendant, the Lord Jesus. "The LORD gives victory to his anointed" (20:6) foreshadows how God would protect Jesus and ultimately give Him all authority (Matthew 28:18).

The psalm concludes with the people confessing that their trust is in God's power and not in human strength (Psalm 20:7).

The songs of the book of Revelation, like Psalm 20, rejoice in the triumph of the king. Paradoxically, the true king, Jesus, won His battle by being slain. The saints in heaven rejoice because they share in His victory; "You have made them to be a kingdom and priests to serve our God, and they will reign on the earth" (Revelation 5:10).

Our King will march out in battle one more time, leading the armies of heaven when "with justice he judges and wages war" (Revelation 19:11–18). Since He is the Lord's anointed, we know God will give victory to this king (Psalm 20:9). We know He will answer us when we call, and our prayer is, "Come, Lord Jesus."

ThinkThrough

How should we be praying for those the Lord has placed in authority over us?

What are some of the "horses" and "chariots" that we can be tempted to trust in, rather than "the name of the LORD our God" (Psalm 20:7)?

Day 21

Read Psalm 21

In Psalm 20, God's people prayed that the Lord would give their king his heart's desire (v. 4) and victory in battle (v. 5). The rest of the psalm was David's confident reply that the Lord "gives victory to his anointed" (v. 6). Now, in Psalm 21, David thanks God for answering this prayer. He rejoices that "you have granted him his heart's desire" (v. 2) and, "through the victories you gave, his glory is great" (v. 5).

The psalm is in two parts. In verses 1 to 7, David is thankful to God for what He has done. He has given him rich, unending blessings, kingship, long life, victory in battle, and "made him glad with the joy of your presence" (v. 6). David knows that these blessings are the result of a relationship between God and him. From David's end, he has continued to "[trust] in the LORD" (v. 7). On God's part, which is the foundation of the relationship, "through the unfailing love of the Most High" (v. 7) David rests secure.

In the second part of the psalm (vv. 8–12), David speaks confidently of what God will do in the future, when He finally puts an end to all His enemies.

Psalm 21 is about God's king rejoicing in the Lord's strength. We can identify with much that David sings about. The Lord has blessed us abundantly, given us long life—eternal life even—and made us glad with the joy of His presence. But more than that, this psalm describes God's goodness to His anointed king.

Now, read this psalm again. As you do, see how all these words will be perfectly fulfilled in the Lord Jesus. He knows joy in His Father's presence, deeper than any other person. God has placed on His head a crown; indeed, on Jesus' head are many crowns (Revelation 19:12). One day, all His enemies will be destroyed, "for he must reign until he has put all his enemies under his feet" (1 Corinthians 15:25).

Where are you and I in Psalm 21? **We are the wonderful benefactors of all God's blessings to His king. Our loving Lord won all these victories for us!** So, Jesus invites us to "come and share your master's happiness" (Matthew 25:21).

ThinkThrough

Meditate on Psalm 21, and make a note of how all the blessings of this ancient Israelite king are fulfilled in the Lord Jesus.

Now, think about how we, as disciples of Jesus, share in each of these blessings.

Day 22

Read Psalm 22:1–11

The change in tone from Psalm 21 to Psalm 22 is stunning. Psalm 21 ends with David and his people singing, "we will sing and praise your might" (v. 13), while Psalm 22 begins with David's awful lament: "My God, my God, why have you forsaken me?" (v. 1).

It is no accident that Psalm 22 follows Psalm 21. It has been deliberately placed here to remind us that the triumphs of the king were not without enormous personal cost. We saw how Psalm 21 points forward to Jesus, and we see this even more clearly in Psalm 22. In fact, no other psalm is as vivid in describing the suffering of the Lord Jesus on the cross.

Psalm 22 is the story of the king's journey from despair to deliverance. In the first part, David expresses his deep and painful sense that God has forsaken him. What can make suffering so difficult is that what we know about God rescuing His people doesn't seem to be real in our lives. We read stories of God wonderfully rescuing His people, and then wonder why the Lord has deserted us (vv. 4–5).

As Jesus suffered on the cross, He turned to Psalm 22 to express both His sorrow and His hope, crying out: "My God, my God, why have you forsaken me?" (Matthew 27:46). Remarkably, even some of the taunts of the Jewish leaders were prophesied in this psalm. Echoing Psalm 22:8, they mocked: "He trusts in God. Let God rescue him now if he wants him" (Matthew 27:43).

However, it is in the cry of desolation that Psalm 22 speaks most powerfully of Jesus' suffering. While He was still aware that God was His Father (e.g. Luke 23:34, 46) and He knew that He would rise again, Jesus' sense of being abandoned by God was real and horrible. For a time, in a way we'll never understand, the Son who from eternity had known the abiding presence and perfect love of His Father, lost all sense of God's presence.

The wonderful news of the gospel is that Jesus was forsaken so that we may never be abandoned by God. **God turned His face away from Jesus so that He might turn His face towards us in forgiveness, mercy, and love.**

ThinkThrough

Have there been times in your life when you have felt abandoned by God? What comfort can Psalm 22 bring at such times?

In what ways was Jesus' sense of being abandoned by God different from ours?

Day 23

Read Psalm 22:12–31

Psalm 22 is such a remarkable prophecy about the sufferings of Jesus on the cross, we can forget that when David wrote this song he was describing his own life. He often felt that "many bulls surround me" (v. 12), referring to his enemies, and that God had laid him in the dust of death (v. 15).

Verses 12 to 21 continue with a description of David's sufferings. As he describes his physical, emotional, and mental torment, we can compare them with the Gospels' accounts and see how David's words point forward to the death of the Lord Jesus.

David's enemies are described as surrounding him (v. 12), taunting him (v. 13), and abusing his body (vv. 13–14; see John 19:1–3). His throat is parched, he cries out in thirst (Psalm 22:15; see John 19:28–29), and his enemies cast lots for his garments (Psalm 22:18; see John 19:23–24). In the end, he commits himself to the only One who can deliver him (Psalm 22:19–21; see Luke 23:46).

The rest of Psalm 22 describes the rescue, vindication, and glorification of the king. We can be sure that just as Jesus remembered—in pain—the opening verses of Psalm 22, He took comfort also from the hope of its closing words.

David knows that he will again "declare your name to my people" (v. 22). His rescue by God means blessing and salvation for the people under his rule. He says "the poor will eat and be satisfied" (v. 26; see Luke 4:18) and "those who seek the Lord will praise him" (Psalm 22:26). This salvation will not just be for Israel in the days of King David, but also for all people for generations to come.

David, who has experienced God's salvation, proclaims the Saviour God to all the ends of the earth, so that "all the families of the nations will bow down before him" (v. 27). Indeed, as Paul reminds us, one day every knee will bow and every tongue confess that Jesus Christ is Lord (Philippians 2:10–11).

Again, this salvation is for all generations to come, including we who live at the beginning of the 21st century. **We, who were for David as yet unborn, have been told about the Lord. We experience His salvation because, in the words of this song's triumphant climax, "He has done it!"** (Psalm 22:31). So we should praise Him!

ThinkThrough

Reflect on the Gospel accounts of Jesus' death on the cross. What evidence can you see that Jesus was confident that the Lord would deliver Him?

In Psalm 22:22–31, David gives us the content of the songs of praise we should sing when we gather. What should be the "theme of [our] praise in the great assembly" (v. 25)? How well do the songs we sing in church reflect the priorities of Psalm 22?

Day 24

Read Psalm 23

For many people, Psalm 23 is their favourite. It is the song of a man characterising himself as a sheep under the watchful, loving eye of his divine shepherd. This shepherd is with him in all circumstances. This is the kind of God we all need and long for.

The poet takes us to three places. The first is beside still waters and in green pastures (v. 2); a picture of serenity and prosperity. While this might seem an idealistic view of life, in the next verse David reminds us that the Lord restores his weary soul (v. 3). This implies there were times when his soul was weighed down and needed restoring. Yet, as David looks back on his life, his overwhelming testimony is that God has been good to him.

At the end of the stanza David moves from the world of metaphors—green pastures and still waters—to the world of everyday moral choices. He is aware that God has kept him on the path of righteousness, causing him to love and obey His commands (v. 3).

David then remembers the hard times, and he takes us to the second place, "the darkest valley" of the shadow of death (v. 4). Notice he does not say that in this valley he was never hurt, attacked, or insulted. The one thing he affirms is that he doesn't fear any evil. David knew fear (e.g. 18:6; 56:3), but he does not fear that his shepherd has abandoned him in this valley.

In the final stanza, David is a guest at his Lord's table. This picture of sharing a meal with God is a lovely portrait of kindness and intimacy. Finally, David expresses confidence in God's longing to continually bless him with goodness and mercy, knowing that he will dwell in the presence of his loving Lord forever.

This is a marvellous picture of God's relationship, not just with David, but also with you and me. We all can have a deeply personal relationship with Jesus, the Good Shepherd (John 10:2–16). One day, Jesus saw the crowds, harassed and helpless, sat them down on a green pasture, and fed them (Mark 6:34–44). This Good Shepherd calmed a terrifying storm and it became still waters (Matthew 8:23–27). Our shepherd laid down His life for His sheep, so that in Paradise we might dwell in His house forever.

ThinkThrough

Why does the Bible regularly choose the picture of a shepherd and sheep to describe God's relationship with His people?

The Lord Jesus regularly had meals with sinners (e.g. Mark 2:15). What does sharing a meal with others say about our relationship with them? When God prepares a table for us (Psalm 23:5), what does it say about His relationship with us?

Day 25

Read Psalm 24

Psalm 23 ends with the confident words of David, that he would "dwell in the house of the LORD for ever" (v. 6). How does David know that? Who are those who will dwell in the house of the Lord forever? In three magnificent parts, Psalm 24 answers that question.

The psalm begins with praising God, who has made everything (vv. 1–2). We put borders around the land and call them our countries. We put fences around property and call them our homes. We call animals our pets and we put them in our zoos. Ultimately, however, everything belongs to God. Therefore, everything owes Him honour, praise, and glory (see Revelation 4:11).

In the next stanza, the psalmist asks: Who can enter the presence of a holy God (Psalm 24:3)? The answer is: the man or woman with clean hands and a pure heart (v. 4). The clean hands are the outward expression of the pure heart. Jesus said: "Blessed are the pure in heart, for they will see God" (Matthew 5:8). In the context of this psalm, the one with a pure heart is the one who does not trust in an idol (Psalm 24:4). Since God made everything, He alone deserves our trust and worship.

The God of Israel lives in "the highest heaven" (see 1 Kings 8:27). Symbolically, however, He lived among His people in the temple on His holy hill. David had just sung about the coming of God's pure people to God's holy mountain. Now, he sings of God coming to meet His people (Psalm 24:7–10). The people, symbolised by their city gates, lift their hands, hearts, and voices to welcome their all-conquering king.

But this was not the only time the people welcomed their king into the city. Centuries later, the Lord came in a manger in Bethlehem to bring salvation from our enemies (Luke 1:68–71). Then, the people welcomed their king with songs of Hosanna as He rode into Jerusalem. This king would fight and win His greatest battle over sin and death on the mountain of the Lord. Finally, this king of glory will come again to win the last battle. This song, which celebrates the coming of the king, points to the first and second comings of Jesus.

Today, let us give God all the praise He deserves. **Let us resolve to keep our hearts pure, and to serve Him alone. Let us be ready to meet the all-conquering king of glory when He comes to His people.**

ThinkThrough

What does knowing that "the earth is the LORD's, and everything in it" (Psalm 24:1) mean for you personally?

What are the idols and false gods that people put their trust in today?

Day 26

Read Psalm 25

Shame is a powerful human emotion. In many cultures, the avoidance of public shame, or the loss of face, shapes human behaviour more than anything else. People will lie, steal, or even kill, rather than suffer shame. David's prayer in Psalm 25 is "do not let me be put to shame" (v. 2).

Once again, the context of this psalm is opposition from David's enemies (vv. 2–3, 19), but this is not his main concern. More than any shame he would suffer if his enemies triumphed over him, David fears shame before God. In the Old Testament, shame "refers primarily to the objective ruin of the evildoer".[6] David repeatedly asks God not to remember his sins (vv. 7, 11, 18). His commitment is to keep his eyes always on the Lord (v. 15) and to continue keeping the demands of His covenant (v. 10).

Notice, first, the importance of confession and repentance. David does not hide his sins, but asks the Lord to take them away (vv. 7, 11, 18). The public and private confession of our sins needs to be a regular Christian practice. **When we forget our need for forgiveness, we forget the wonder of God's grace.**

Secondly, David asks the Lord to "teach me your paths" (vv. 4, 9, 12). He knows he needs God's wisdom, revealed in the Scriptures, to continue to obey Him and remain in His love.

Thirdly, lying behind everything David writes here are the terms of God's covenant with Israel. Should His people continue to obey Him, the Lord will maintain steadfast love and faithfulness, forgive their sins, and protect them from their enemies (Exodus 34). David knows that there are two sides to a covenant. God will be faithful and protect His servant, but His servant must himself be faithful. So, David sings: "May integrity and uprightness protect me, because my hope, Lord, is in you" (Psalm 25:21, see v. 10).

Writing to the Philippians from a prison cell, Paul had a similar prayer. His hope was "that I will in no way be ashamed" (Philippians 1:20). Surrounded by enemies, Paul sought to remain faithful in his life and witness. More than human abuse, he dreaded standing before his Lord, ashamed that he had not kept the faith. Both Paul and David knew that this was the shame to be avoided, and so both put their trust in God.

[6] Dictionary of New Testament Theology, vol. 3, s.v. "shame".

ThinkThrough

Why can David be confident that God will not remember the sins of his youth (Psalm 25:6–7)? Why can we as Christians have an even greater confidence in the Lord's forgiveness?

What does Psalm 25 teach us about the character of God? What confidence does this give David in what he asks from the Lord?

Day 27

Read Psalm 26

It has been said: "Christians are not perfect, just forgiven." Certainly no one is perfect, but we are more than "just forgiven". When God forgives us and justifies us, He gives us His Holy Spirit. God's Spirit then begins the work of sanctifying us. We are being renewed inwardly daily (2 Corinthians 4:16) and being conformed to the likeness of Jesus (Romans 8:29). We are changed people, although we still await our complete transformation in the age to come.

In Psalm 25, David asked God to protect him because he had lived a life of integrity (v. 21). This did not mean he was without sin (see v. 18), but that he had lived a life of consistent obedience. He continues this theme in Psalm 26. David's life is an open book before God, and he has a clear conscience, for "I have trusted in the LORD and have not faltered" (v. 1). David's assertion should also be found on the lips of Christians, who are called to be "blameless" (e.g. Philippians 2:14–15) and to trust in God.

In Psalm 1, God blesses the righteous person who does not "sit in the company of mockers" (v. 1). This is David's claim in Psalm 26: he does not sit with the wicked (v. 5). In other words, he has not participated in their sinful behaviour.

David's obedience is much more than outward conformity to the Law. It springs from a heart of love. He knows the Lord loves him (v. 3), and he loves and glories in living in the presence of his God (v. 8). The bedrock of David's confidence in his salvation is God's faithfulness (v. 3).

We have the same assurance. **God has promised to give eternal life to those who trust in the saving work of the Lord Jesus. We can trust God will be faithful to this promise.** Along with that, like David, we who have lived with a clear conscience can know that God will reward our faithfulness (see 2 Timothy 4:7–8).

David claimed to "have not faltered" in his life (Psalm 26:1), but we know he still sinned, sometimes terribly. Psalm 26 reminds us of the greater king who, although tempted in every way, never sinned (Hebrews 4:15). It is only to the Lord Jesus that the words David sings here fully apply.

ThinkThrough

As you reflect on Psalm 26, ask the Lord to "examine my heart and my mind" (v. 2). Is there something you need to do so that you can live before the Lord with a clear conscience?

"LORD, I love the house where you live" (v. 8). Paul tells us that the church, God's people, are His house (1 Corinthians 3:16). How do David's words help us to appreciate the glory of the church? How can they challenge our attitude towards the church?

Day 28

Read Psalm 27

My daughter's uncle asked her one time what she looked for in a husband. Pippa replied: "A man who loves God more than he loves me." What a wonderful answer! The greatest commandment is to love the Lord your God with all your heart and mind (Matthew 22:37–38), and the first mark of genuine faith is a deep love of the Lord. In Psalm 27, David beautifully expresses his love for God.

Psalm 27 continues, and develops, some of the themes we saw in Psalms 25 and 26. David longs to know God's ways so he can please Him in all he does (25:4–5), and he rejoices in being in the house of God (26:8).

The psalm opens with David expressing his confidence in God's protection (27:1–3). Using military metaphors ("the stronghold of my life"), he declares that God will protect him, both on the battlefield and throughout his life.

At the centre of Israel's life was the tabernacle and later, the temple where the Lord made His home. David longs to live with his God forever. Paul expresses the same passion for his Saviour when he writes: "I consider everything a loss because of the surpassing worth of knowing Christ Jesus my Lord" (Philippians 3:8). This leads David to spontaneous praise: "I will sing and make music to the Lord" (Psalm 27:6).

This has been the experience of many believers throughout history. **Once we understand the depth of God's love for us, we naturally sing.** We don't sing just because God commands it (e.g. Psalm 9:11), but also because the wonders of God's salvation, protection, presence, and beauty demand more than sermons and studies. That is why, at the heart of our Bible, is the church's songbook.

Psalm 27 is the song of a man whose heart has been captured by God, whose heart calls out to God: "Seek his face" (v. 8). What the heart desires, the will pursues. So David responds: "Your face, Lord, I will seek" (v. 8). David longs for this deep encounter with God, and knows he will find it: God will not reject him (vv. 9–10). However, he knows that he needs to wait until that day when he—and we—fully behold the face of God (vv. 13–14).

ThinkThrough

Why do Christians sing? What part do the Psalms play in worship in your church?

God has promised: "Never will I leave you" (Hebrews 13:5). Is it still appropriate for Christians to ask of the Lord: "Do not reject me or forsake me" (Psalm 27:9)? Why or why not?

Day 29

Read Psalm 28

An "eye for eye" (Exodus 21:24) is a core principle of biblical justice. In other words, let the punishment fit the crime. Sadly, in a sinful world, the innocent are often punished while the guilty escape or are treated too leniently. In such a world, Christians turn to the Judge of all the earth to "repay them for their deeds" (Psalm 28:4).

We can't be sure what event in David's life this psalm is speaking about, although it fits neatly with the account of the murder of Abner by David's commander-in-chief Joab. Abner had been Saul's closest supporter and had led the pursuit of David. After Saul's death, war broke out between David and Saul's son, Ishbosheth. During the battle, Abner reluctantly killed Joab's brother, Asahel (2 Samuel 2:18–28). Later, Abner made peace with David. But Joab wanted revenge for the death of his brother and, by deceit, murdered Abner (3:27).

The tragic events of this story can be heard in the words of Psalm 28. David sings that the wicked "speak cordially with their neighbours but harbour malice in their hearts" (v. 3). This is precisely what Joab did when he invited Abner into his chamber for a private conversation, intending murder (2 Samuel 3:27). David then proclaimed he was innocent of the blood of Abner, and that Joab and his family should bear the consequences of their evil actions (vv. 28–29). In this psalm David sings: "Do not drag me away with the wicked . . . repay them for what their hands have done" (Psalm 28:3–4).

Why do the wicked do evil deeds? David's answer is: "Because they have no regard for the deeds of the Lord" (v. 5). When we forget God's deeds of judgment, we stop fearing Him and are easily tempted to evil actions. When we forget how God has shown His love for us, we begin to neglect deeds of love. For this reason Jesus taught: "You have heard that it was said, 'Eye for eye' . . . but I tell you . . . turn to them the other cheek" (Matthew 5:38–39). **While we still call out to God for justice, we who are forgiven sinners pursue peace, love, and mercy in our relationships.**

ThinkThrough

What are the great deeds of God that we should give regard to (Psalm 28:5)? What impact should reflecting on these deeds have on how we live?

Psalm 28 moves from petition ("hear my cry for mercy", v. 2) to thanksgiving ("he has heard my cry for mercy", v. 6). What has led David to be so confident that God has heard him?

Day 30

Read Psalm 29

My wife loves storms. When the lightning flashes, the thunder crashes, and the rain batters the roof, Sarah's heart leaps with joy and wonder. Yet storms can also be terrifying. At the crash of thunder, children run to their parents for safety, and animals howl in fear. Psalm 29 is a majestic invitation to worship the powerful God of creation.

David begins by calling on the heavenly beings to "worship the LORD in the splendour of his holiness" (v. 2). He then takes us on a tour of the awesome character of God's world (vv. 3–9). As you read this psalm, try to picture in your mind's eye what David describes. See the mighty oceans, the trees of Lebanon which were famous in the ancient world for their size and strength, the mountains of Lebanon and Sirion (which is Mount Hermon), the storm, the desert, the animals (verse 9 is sometimes translated as "the voice of the Lord made the deer give birth"), and the forests.

Above all this, Psalm 29 is a psalm in praise of God's voice, which rules His world. Seven times David describes the power of God's voice (vv. 3–9). From the seven days of creation to the cycles of seven throughout the book of Revelation, seven in the Bible is the number of completeness or perfection. In other words, all power is found in the voice of God. The cedars of Lebanon are imposing and majestic, but they crumble at God's voice (v. 5). God's voice sends the thunder and the desert storm, and "strips the forests bare" (vv. 7–9).

The natural response to seeing the power of God over creation is fear. Yet, that is not the note on which the psalm concludes. **We, as God's people, take comfort from knowing that the Lord uses all this power for our good.** He gives us His strength and blesses us with peace (vv. 10–11).

Psalm 29 invites us to open our eyes and behold God's power all around us. Look at a mighty river or sea. Stand in wonder at a storm. Gaze up at a towering mountain. Behold the vastness of a forest. Then rejoice, that the same power that controls them blesses you with peace, "and the peace of God, which transcends all understanding, will guard your hearts and your minds in Christ Jesus" (Philippians 4:7).

ThinkThrough

How can we, both as individuals and as a church, "ascribe to the LORD glory and strength" (Psalm 29:1)?

Can you recall times in your life when you were struck by the power of God in creation? How did they lead you to "ascribe to the LORD the glory due to his name" (v. 2)?

Day 31

Read Psalm 30

Sometimes, Christians are asked to give their testimony. This might be a simple conversation with a friend or a short talk in church. In our testimony we often speak of our hard times or even our failures. However, the main theme of a Christian's testimony should be the goodness and grace of God, and of how, through the good and bad times, "You turned my wailing into dancing" (Psalm 30:11).

We are told that David wrote this psalm for the dedication of the temple. Of course, it was his son, Solomon, who built and dedicated the temple (1 Kings 8), so perhaps David first sang this psalm as he brought the ark into Jerusalem and danced before the Lord (2 Samuel 6:12–15).

David begins by exalting—lifting up—the Lord, because the Lord has lifted him up (Psalm 30:1). God has spared David's life. Is David referring to a life-threatening illness ("and you healed me", v. 2) or the attacks of his enemies (v. 1)? Perhaps it is both. His testimony is that God has saved his life, and he invites Israel to praise God with him.

David does not hide his faults. He had experienced God's anger, presumably for his sin (v. 5). There was also a time when success had made him complacent in his spiritual life (v. 6). God shook him out of his complacency by turning His face away from him (v. 7). David's testimony, though, is that God's anger lasts only for a moment, while His grace is eternal.

What a wonderful truth to hold on to! Some time ago, a man confessed to me that he hadn't been to church for seven years because he felt so guilty for a sin he had committed. He felt that God's anger lasts a lifetime. No. It passes like the night, and then we awake into the sunlight of His grace (v. 5).

In many Christian traditions, Psalm 30 is read at Easter. The great church leader, St. Augustine, believed the psalm sang of "the joy of the resurrection".[7] But there is no resurrection without a cross, just as there is no day without night.

David knew wailing, but his testimony is that God's grace turns tears into songs.

[7] Augustine, "Exposition on Psalm 30", in Nicene and Post-Nicene Fathers, ed. Philip Schaff, first series, vol. 8 (Buffalo, NY: Christian Literature Publishing, 1888).

ThinkThrough

What testimony would you give of God's saving grace?

What factors can lead to our spiritual complacency? How do we protect ourselves against this?

Day 32

Read Psalm 31

1 Samuel 23 describes a time when David, on the run from King Saul, rescued the town of Keilah in Judah, which was being besieged by the Philistines. On hearing that David was there, Saul went to find him. Through the words of a prophet, David was warned that the people of Keilah, whom he'd come to save, would betray him. So he fled into the Desert of Ziph, where Saul's son, Jonathan, "helped him to find strength in God" (1 Samuel 23:16) and assured him he would be king. However, the Ziphites also planned to hand David over to Saul. At the moment he was closing in on David, Saul heard of another raid by the Philistines, and had to break off his pursuit.

According to 1 Samuel 23, David suffered betrayals, traps, and near escapes from death. But above all else, he experienced the protection of God. It is probable that Psalm 31 is recalling these events. David remembers how God showed him the wonders of His love, "when I was in a city under siege" (v. 21). In utter despair, he recalls the plots to take his life (vv. 4, 9–13). In the midst of his laments, however, there are repeated expressions of trust in God, and a confidence that God will deliver him (vv. 19–24).

While most of us will never have to suffer the kind of trials David endured, we can learn from his experiences. **David's example encourages us to "love the Lord" even in the dark days, for "the Lord preserves those who are true to him"** (v. 23). When we are in distress and our eyes grow weak with sorrow (v. 9), we can find refuge in God our rock.

According to the Gospel of Luke, the last words Jesus spoke before He died were: "Father, into your hands I commit my spirit" (Luke 23:46). With His final breath, Jesus remembered Psalm 31:5. On the cross, Jesus would have considered how those He came to save had betrayed Him. And while God rescued David from his enemies, He allowed Jesus to be handed over to His enemies. God did this so that the promises of Psalm 31, made to David and to us, might be fulfilled: that we would enjoy the abundance of good things God has stored up for us (v. 19).

ThinkThrough

Reflect on the times in your life when you were greatly distressed. What comfort and help does Psalm 31 bring to people who are in despair?

Why do you think the Lord Jesus chose to quote Psalm 31 as He breathed His last breath?

Day 33

Read Psalm 32

How often do you confess your sins? Every day? Once a week? Once a month? Never? Regular confession of sin is a good Christian discipline. It keeps us humble and reminds us that we are sinners who have been saved by grace.

The book of Psalms began with the pronouncement of blessing on the righteous person who does not participate in the sins of the ungodly (1:1). Sadly, God's people sometimes fail, and now, David pronounces another blessing: blessed are those whose sins are forgiven.

David does not provide us with any details of the sin that prompted this heartfelt psalm of repentance. For a while, though, he tried to hide the sin from God (Psalm 32:3). Unconfessed sin can impact our mental, emotional, and physical well-being (vv. 3–4). Only confession, and then knowing the joy of full forgiveness, can bring healing and restoration (v. 5).

While we, like David, rejoice in God's forgiveness, we must never forget the price God paid. Our sins aren't counted against us (v. 2) because they were counted against Jesus in our place. That is why Paul quotes Psalm 32:1–2 in his letter to the Romans to prove that salvation is by faith in Christ alone, and not works (Romans 4:4–8).

In the rest of the psalm David tells us, when we sin, to follow his example and pray to God, "while you may be found" (Psalm 32:6). Only a stubborn mule would ignore God's Word, which teaches us the way of obedience and the remedy for sin. God's forgiven people don't experience His wrath; instead, they are surrounded by "the LORD's unfailing love" (v. 10).

Godly believers still sin, but confess their sin. Faithful Christians find wisdom for living in God's Word. Whenever we open the Bible, God says to us: "I will counsel you with my loving eye on you" (v. 8). The righteous sing songs of joy, and their greatest song is in praise of sins forgiven (v. 11).

Psalm 32 was one of church father St. Augustine's favourite psalms. It's been said that he couldn't read it without tears in his eyes, and before he died he had the words of the psalm written on the wall by his bed. It would be a wonderful psalm to keep close to us as well.

ThinkThrough

How have you seen or experienced the damage that unconfessed sin can do to people?

What does David mean when he tells us to pray to God, "while you may be found" (Psalm 32:6)? Is there a warning here for us, as well as a promise?

Day 34

Read Psalm 33

Songs of praise have been compared to advertising. An advertisement tells people how good the product is and why they should buy it. Similarly, our songs describe and promote the glories of God, and declare and celebrate His wonderful deeds. There is a place to simply "praise the Lord" (for example, Psalm 150), but usually the Psalms tell us why God is worthy of our praise. When we sing, we advertise God's character and His works. We see that in Psalm 33.

Psalm 33 has no title, so it is probably a continuation of Psalm 32. Psalm 32 ended with the invitation: "Sing, all you who are upright in heart!" (v. 11). Psalm 33 begins: "Sing joyfully to the LORD, you righteous."

Psalm 33 is very carefully composed. In Hebrew, there are 161 words in the psalm. The middle word, the 81st, is "blessed" (v. 12). Psalm 33 explains why God's people are blessed and should sing a new song to Him (v. 3).

We should praise the Lord because He is "faithful in all he does" (v. 4). In other words, everything God does is for the good of those who trust in Him. We rejoice because "the earth is full of his unfailing love" (v. 5). Because of what Jesus has done for us, Christians know—even more than the people of ancient Israel—the length and breadth of the Father's love for us. We sing because God protects His people. Just as His powerful word controls the seas, so He rules and controls the nations. These nations may plot against the Lord and His people, but we are secure in Him (vv. 10–11).

The psalmist twice rejoices that the Lord sees everything (vv. 13–15). God observes everything that everyone does. These same all-seeing eyes watch over all those "whose hope is in his unfailing love" (vv. 18–20). Sandwiched between these two passages is a word of assurance: it is the God who sees from heaven who is to be trusted, not armies or human strength (vv. 16–17).

Who are these people who sing joyfully? They are His inheritance (v. 12). All God's wonderful future plans are focused on the blessings He will shower on His people. These people are "those who fear him . . . whose hope is in his unfailing love" (v. 18). Fear and love are not enemies, but two sides of the character of men and women whose trust is in this awesome God, who is worthy of our praise.

ThinkThrough

Read Psalm 33 again and make a list of all the reasons we are given to sing joyfully to the Lord.

In verse 18, we see that the Lord's eyes are on those who both fear God and experience His love. How can it be that fearing and loving God are two necessary and compatible ways to respond to the Lord?

Day 35

Read Psalm 34

One of the encouraging features of singing is that it is one of the few things we can all do together as a church. God's Word is proclaimed by the preacher. Normally, someone leads the church in prayer. But singing is one dimension of public worship in which we all participate. In Paul's words, we teach and admonish one another with all wisdom through psalms, hymns, and spiritual songs (Colossians 3:16).

In the heading for Psalm 34 we are told that David composed this song after he pretended to be mad, and so escaped from the Philistines (see 1 Samuel 21:10–22:1). While on the run from Saul, David took refuge in a Philistine city, feigning insanity so they wouldn't kill him. While this clever subterfuge was successful, David recognised that God was his true deliverer.

We, too, can testify to times when the Lord has come to our help. So, David invites us to sing with him: "Let us exalt his name together" (Psalm 34:3). It's a joyful, confident assertion that "the LORD will rescue his servants" (v. 22). This is the main theme of the song.

In 1 Peter we see again how important the Psalms were to the writers of the New Testament. Citing Psalm 34:8—"Taste and see that the LORD is good"—Peter reminds us in 1 Peter 2:3 that we have come to know salvation through God's Word that's been preached to us. He encourages us to mature as disciples by craving the milk of God's Word (v. 2) as we express our salvation in the way we live (v. 1). Psalm 34 makes the same point: God has been good to us in saving us, so we respond to His kindness by turning from evil and doing good (v. 14).

Psalm 34 also contains a prophecy about Jesus' death. The apostle John saw Jesus being crucified and observed that, despite the custom of breaking legs to hasten death, the soldiers did not break Jesus' bones. Citing Psalm 34:20, John says: "These things happened so that the scripture would be fulfilled: 'Not one of his bones will be broken'" (John 19:36). God rescued His righteous servant David by keeping him from death. This points forward to the greater rescue of His perfectly righteous servant and son, Jesus, whom God raised from the dead.

Today, let us sing with David because God has rescued us and made our faces radiant (Psalm 34:5) with the joy of salvation.

ThinkThrough

What kind of image does the verse "taste and see that the LORD is good" (Psalm 34:8) bring to your mind as you consider your relationship with God?

David sings that God delivers us from all troubles. How can we apply this truth when we meet trouble, suffering, and persecution in our lives?

Day 36

Read Psalm 35

Sometimes, our troubles seem never-ending. There may be a family member, a neighbour, or a co-worker who, despite all the good you do for them, continues trying to make your life as difficult as possible.

There were times when David must have felt that his troubles would never end. It is possible that Saul relentlessly pursued David for as long as seven or eight years to kill him. David had done nothing to hurt Saul. In fact, he remained loyal to this wicked king. Yet, Saul and many with him repaid David's kindness by plotting his ruin (Psalm 35:4).

There are three parts to Psalm 35 (vv. 1–10, 11–18, 19–28). In the first, David repeatedly pleads with God to intervene and rescue him. He asks for justice, which is essentially giving people what they deserve. The innocent deserve acquittal. The guilty deserve punishment. For example, David prays about those who have dug a pit for him to fall into, saying: "May they fall into the pit, to their ruin" (v. 8). David rightly understands the true character of justice and vengeance. He recognises that it is for God alone to exact vengeance, and leaves justice to Him (v. 23).

The second part is the most heart-breaking (vv. 11–18). The people who hate David and have turned against him are those he once considered friends. He loved them and cared for them: "When they were ill, I put on sackcloth" (v. 13). Now, they slander him and gloat over his distress (vv. 15, 19, 24, 26).

In the third part, David looks to the Lord for vindication (v. 24). He asks that God "put to shame" those who have treated him so cruelly (v. 26). One can feel David's anger in this psalm. It hurts so much when people to whom you have been kind, treat you so badly. This is a righteous anger in tune with the heart of God. Jesus displayed this kind of anger at the religious leaders who opposed Him despite the good He had done (e.g. Mark 3:1–5).

It is important to note, though, how each section of this psalm ends: "Then my soul will rejoice in the LORD" (Psalm 35:9); "I will give you thanks in the great assembly" (v. 18); "My tongue will proclaim your righteousness, your praises all day long" (v. 28). **We suffer injustice and, appropriately, we may be hurt and angry, but we never cease to trust and praise God, who will punish the guilty and vindicate the innocent.**

ThinkThrough

Can you think of times when you felt like David in Psalm 35? How did you respond to those who wronged you? In the light of this psalm, how might you have responded differently?

Christians believe in a final judgment. How does such a belief impact how we might apply this psalm today?

Day 37

Read Psalm 36

Karl Marx, the philosopher whose writings gave rise to communism, once wrote that religion is the opium of the people. He meant that people take religion as a drug to escape the reality of life's hardships, as it gives them the delusion that they will die and go to a place called heaven.

Marx was wrong. Polish poet and Nobel Prize winner Czeslaw Milosz, who had actually lived under the atheistic regimes of Nazism and communism, said that the true opium of people is the belief that there is nothing after death. People foolishly pretend that God will not judge them for all their betrayals, greed, cowardice, and murder. In Psalm 36, David reaches the same conclusion as Milosz.

David begins this psalm with an observation about sin. He recognises that the root of all sin is a failure to fear God (v. 1). It is a rejection of the truth that God will judge us. These same words are used to form the conclusion to Paul's devastating critique of human sin in Romans 1–3. Paul demonstrates that everyone has sinned, and therefore everyone needs the salvation that is found only in Jesus. Paul concludes by quoting Psalm 36:1: "There is no fear of God before their eyes" (Romans 3:18).

David goes on to say that people not only fail to fear God, but also delude themselves into thinking they are basically good (Psalm 36:2). Nothing has changed. **Most people will claim that they are good people, and that their good deeds will save them if there really is a Judgment Day.** As David says: "The words of their mouths are wicked and deceitful" (v. 3).

In Romans 3, Paul moves from the "bad news" of human sin to the "good news" of God's love in sending Jesus to atone for our sin. Psalm 36 follows the same pattern. The rest of the psalm is a wonderful celebration of God's love and righteousness, which "reaches to the heavens" (v. 5). Jesus said that He came to give us abundant life (John 10:10). In David's words, we "drink from your river of delights" (Psalm 36:8). In his letter to the Romans, Paul goes on to describe some of these delights: peace with God; God's love poured into our hearts; our adoption as sons; and more than conquerors (Romans 5:1, 5; 8:15–16, 37).

Psalm 36 should make us exalt in the riches we have in Jesus, and pray for those we know who don't fear God.

ThinkThrough

Why do many churches talk so little of "the fear of God" when the Bible speaks so much about it? What are some of the consequences of failing to understand the fear of the Lord?

While rejoicing in God's love and justice, why do you think David speaks of God preserving "both people and animals" (Psalm 36:6)? Today, make Psalm 36:10 the basis of a prayer for yourself and others.

Day 38

Read Psalm 37

There is a famous saying that "crime does not pay". Is that true? It depends on your perspective. If this life is all there is, then clearly a life of crime often pays. Many criminals escape punishment, become wealthy, and live long lives. On the other hand, many good people never see worldly wealth and die young. However, if death is the great inescapable reality and afterwards comes judgment and eternity, then "the wicked will be no more" and the meek will enjoy peace and prosperity (Psalm 37:10–11).

We saw that Psalm 1 begins the book of Psalms by contrasting the character and destiny of the righteous and the wicked. Psalm 37 develops these themes.

Its opening verses begin and end with an exhortation not to fret over or envy the apparent success of the wicked (vv. 1, 7). It is easy to be angry at the injustice when, despite your loyalty and integrity, a colleague who is lazy or dishonest is promoted over you. But remember, says David, "like the grass they will soon wither" (v. 2; see vv. 10, 13, 15, 17, 20, 22, 28, 34, 36). The righteous are to keep living lives of faith and goodness, delighting in the Lord. As Peter writes about our faith in Jesus, "you believe in him and are filled with an inexpressible and glorious joy" (1 Peter 1:8).

If we are not careful, we can let bitterness and resentment consume us when we see the success of the wicked. Instead, David calls us to "be still . . . and wait patiently for him" (Psalm 37:7). Long for and pray for the day when your righteous reward will shine like the dawn (v. 6). This is repeatedly described by David in terms of the righteous inheriting the land (vv. 3, 9, 11, 18, 22, 27, 29, 34). Jesus quoted verse 11 in the beatitudes when He pronounced that we, His disciples, are blessed, for "the meek will inherit the land" (v. 11; see Matthew 5:5).

We have the certain hope of the new creation where we will enjoy "the things God has prepared for those who love him" (1 Corinthians 2:9). In a rebellious world filled with injustice, God calls on us to keep the faith and remember that the Lord "knows their day is coming" (Psalm 37:13).

ThinkThrough

Can you think of times when you fretted over the prosperity of the wicked? How did you deal with these feelings?

What do you think David means when he tells us to "be still" (Psalm 37:7)? Is he telling us to do nothing and be quiet in the face of injustice? Or is there a more active kind of stillness?

Day 39

Read Psalm 38

Many churches no longer practise the public confession of sin. This is a significant loss. Whenever we come together, it is appropriate to remind one another that we gather only by God's grace. He has forgiven us and made it possible for us to enter His presence. Regular corporate confession also gives people an opportunity to acknowledge that they have sinned, whether it is by doing what they should not have done, or not doing what they should have.

Psalm 38 is another one of David's laments over sin. As with Psalm 32, we don't know the circumstances of David's sin. Was it his adultery with Bathsheba (2 Samuel 11), or his faithless taking of a census (2 Samuel 24)? Perhaps it is not identified so that we can apply David's words to our own situation. Our sins might be different, but the consequences are universal.

Initially, David is acutely aware of God's anger at his sin (Psalm 38:1) and is burdened with guilt (v. 4). Both are appropriate responses to sin. However, unlike David, we should not let such guilt overwhelm us (v. 4). Without for a moment minimising the seriousness of sin, or the fact that it may have lasting consequences, we should remember that the blood of Christ is a fountain of cleansing for those who turn to Him (see Zechariah 13:1).

It also appears that David's sense of guilt has affected his physical health. He is suffering from festering sores, back pain, heart palpitations, and general weariness (Psalm 38:5–10). We are holistic beings. When one part of our being is stressed—such as the spiritual, as in David's case—it impacts us mentally and physically.

Finally, David's sin has provided an opportunity for his enemies to gloat (v. 16). **Sin impacts our Christian witness. People are quick to find inconsistencies in our life and then point out hypocrisy.**

What's the answer for David? Firstly, to be transparent before God: "I confess my iniquity" (v. 18). David gives no excuses for his sin. Secondly, to repent: not only does David turn away from the wrong he has done, but he also commits himself "only to do what is good" (v. 20).

Unlike David, we know the fullness of forgiveness found in Christ. Yet his psalm remains a model for the kind of confession and repentance that God delights in.

ThinkThrough

How might Christians take sin too lightly? What does Psalm 38 teach us about the seriousness of sin?

Do you think there is still a place for the confession of sin when we come together as a church? If so, what is the most helpful way to do this?

Day 40

Read Psalm 39

I live in Melbourne, Australia, where we face the threat of bushfires every summer. It just takes the tiniest spark and a whole forest, including nearby homes, is ablaze. James describes the tongue as a fire (James 3:5–6). A few thoughtless words can cause enormous damage. James advises: "Be quick to listen, slow to speak and slow to become angry" (1:19). This, however, is easier said than done, especially when people speak evil of you. David failed the test of controlling his tongue and this set him on an important journey of self-reflection.

Psalm 39 follows on from the previous psalm of confession. In Psalm 38, we saw his enemies gloating over his sin and suffering (vv. 12, 16). David has tried to hold his tongue but, finally, he can't take it anymore: "My heart grew hot within me . . . then I spoke with my tongue" (39:3).

David scorns those who spend all their days amassing wealth (v. 6), seeing the stupidity of such an existence. First, measured against God's eternity, our life is little more than a brief breath (vv. 4–5). Then, when we die, all our wealth ends up in someone else's pockets (v. 6).

David now comes to the main point of the psalm (v. 7), and he asks the question every man or woman must ask themselves: "What do I look for?" What do I want from life? Wealth? Health? Safety? David knows the answer: "My hope is in you" (v. 7). If this is true, then his biggest problem is his sin, which drives him away from what he most desires: a relationship with God (vv. 10–11).

David's reflections on the brevity of life have made him realise that he's really a foreigner and a stranger in this world. Its values are not his values. Like his ancestors, he realises that this world is not his home. Hebrews alludes to Psalm 39 when it speaks of God's faithful people seeing the fulfilment of all God's promises but only from a distance. They understood that "they were foreigners and strangers on earth" (Hebrews 11:13).

These are the great questions Psalm 39 asks us: What do we long for? Is God for us or against us? Where is our true home?

ThinkThrough

Reflect on the questions Psalm 39 asks: What do you look for? What do you want most from life? Does the way you live express your heart's desire?

Do you sometimes feel like a "foreigner and stranger" in this world (Hebrews 11:13)? What makes you feel that way?

Day 41

Read Psalm 40

If we are honest, some of the troubles we face are of our own making. As David sings: "For troubles without number surround me; my sins have overtaken me" (Psalm 40:12). Sometimes other people caused David sorrow, and sometimes he suffered because of his own sinfulness. In Psalm 40, David rejoices that the Lord has "lifted me . . . out of the mud and mire" (v. 2).

Psalm 40 is a wonderful song of rejoicing in salvation. David sings because the Lord has rescued him from his enemies. But our enemies are both outside of us and within.

David rejoices that he has been delivered from all "who want to take my life" (vv. 14–15), but his greater cause for thanksgiving is God delivering him from an even bigger enemy: the sin in his own heart (vv. 12–13).

Since God has rescued David, he can now sing again, and he delights to tell others of the wonderful works of God (vv. 4–5, 9–10). **Once we have experienced the amazing grace of God in salvation, it is hard to keep it to ourselves.** David cannot conceal God's love and faithfulness from the assembly of God's people (v. 10).

At the heart of this psalm is one of the great spiritual truths of the Bible. God gave His people the sacrificial system. According to the writer of the book of Hebrews, one purpose of these sacrifices was to serve as "an annual reminder of sins" (Hebrews 10:3). The forgiveness a godly Jew experienced from these sacrifices was real, but at the same time he recognised the system's inadequacy. The writer understood that "it is impossible for the blood of bulls and goats to take away sins" (vv. 4, 11), and found support for his argument in Psalm 40:6–8 (see Hebrews 10:5–10). This did not mean that Jews were free from the obligation to fulfil all the laws of sacrifice; rather, godly Jews knew that, more than sacrifice, God demanded obedience.

It is interesting that the writer of Hebrews puts David's words in Psalm 40:6–8 into the mouth of Jesus (Hebrews 10:5–10). When Jesus entered the world, He announced that He had come to do God's will, which was ultimately to bring the complete cleansing from sin that could only be accomplished by His being the one, true sacrifice for sin.

Have you experienced this wonderful deliverance? David prays: "May all who seek you rejoice and be glad in you" (v. 16). You can be sure that if you long for His saving help, you will find that "the Lord is great!" (v. 16).

ThinkThrough

Psalm 40 begins with an encouragement to wait patiently for the Lord (v. 1). What does this mean practically? How did David express his patience for God to deliver him?

God's law required His people to offer sacrifices (e.g. Leviticus 1–7). So how can David say: "Sacrifice and offering you did not desire" (Psalm 40:6)? What principles can we find here for how we live the Christian life?

Day 42

Read Psalm 41

It is a great mistake to think that sickness is always a punishment for sin. Jesus corrected this wrong view (see John 9:1–3). However, it is also a mistake to think that sickness is never a result of sin. Since Psalm 38, David has been thinking about his sinfulness, and has acknowledged that it can have physical consequences (e.g. Psalm 38:3–8). So, when we fall ill, it is wise to search our hearts and see if there is sin that needs to be confessed and repented of.

David has searched his own heart, and admits his sin (41:4). However, sin is both what we do and what we have failed to do. While David acknowledges his sin, one area in which he has maintained integrity is his regard for the weak (v. 1). **If we have not helped the weak in their time of need, how can we call upon God to help us?** David, who presumably is very sick when he writes this psalm, trusts that the Lord will be merciful and restore him (vv. 2–3), just as he has been merciful towards the weak (v. 12).

David's illness had become well known, and he received visitors. Some, though, were hypocritical. In David's presence they pretended to show sorrow and concern. Once they left, they joined his enemies and rejoiced in his condition, confident he would soon die (vv. 5–9). In his gospel, John writes that Psalm 41:9 is fulfilled in the betrayal of Jesus by Judas (John 13:18). He, too, was a friend of the King, the Lord Jesus, and pretended to be loyal. Yet he was conspiring with Jesus' enemies. Here again we see that Jesus and the New Testament writers saw the Old Testament, particularly the Psalms, pointing forward to—and fulfilled in—the life and ministry of Jesus.

Psalm 41 is the conclusion to Book 1 of the five books of Psalms. It concludes on the same note of praise as all five books. Throughout these psalms David has shared his joys and sorrows, his sins and obedience, his times of walking close to God and his times of feeling forsaken. At the end, though, are words of praise: "Praise be to the LORD, the God of Israel, from everlasting to everlasting. Amen and Amen" (v. 13). This is the testimony of every believer.

ThinkThrough

Why does the Bible place such importance on care for the weak and needy? How can we maintain our integrity in this area?

What can we learn from Psalm 41, and other psalms, about a godly response to illness?

Day 43

Read Psalm 42 and 43

Psalms 42 and 43 are very likely to have been originally one psalm. Taken together, the two psalms can be divided into three parts, each concluding with the same chorus: "Why, my soul, are you downcast?" (42:5, 11; 43:5). They are the first psalms of the second book in Psalms (consisting of Psalms 42 to 72), and the first of the psalms attributed to the Sons of Korah, who were probably musicians responsible for worship in the temple.

The two psalms tell the story of a man's sense that God has abandoned him. Psalm 42 begins with the powerful image of a deer lost in the wasteland. It is cut off from the life-giving source of water. The psalmist feels the same sense of desperation. He longs to come back into God's presence (vv. 1–2).

The man is in a foreign land. He is full of sorrow because he cannot participate in the worship that takes place in the temple (vv. 3–4; 43:3). His sense of alienation reaches its lowest point in the second part, when foreigners mock the supposed absence of his God (42:9–10). We see here the struggle in his soul. When we are depressed, our emotions ebb and flow. The psalmist confesses: "My soul is downcast within me" (v. 6, see v. 9), but then he reminds himself: "By day the Lord directs his love, at night his song is with me" (v. 8).

In the third part, the poet longs for God to rescue him (Psalm 43). Again, we are not told what caused this crisis in his life. The details are kept vague so that we, too, can sing this song when the Lord seems far from us. The final verses are words of hope (Psalm 43:3–5). The psalmist is confident that God's light and truth will bring him back to Jerusalem and to God. Again he will praise Him in the assembly of God's people.

Today, we Christians have God's presence by His Spirit everywhere we go. Still, many will testify to times in their lives when God feels distant. Psalms 42 and 43 give us a song to sing at such times, and a reminder that we will return to God, "my joy and my delight" (43:4).

Psalms 42 and 43 describe the experience of one man who felt abandoned by God. They remind us of Jesus, who on the cross experienced even greater abandonment than this man. In Gethsemane He prayed: "My soul is overwhelmed with sorrow to the point of death" (Matthew 26:38). Yet He, too, put His hope in God.

ThinkThrough

Since the Day of Pentecost, God's people have known the presence of God by His Spirit, all the time and everywhere. In our experience of God, what do we share in common with the writer of Psalms 42 and 43, who lived under the old covenant? How is our experience of God's presence different from his?

When he is downcast, the psalmist rebukes himself: "Why are you downcast?" What can we learn from him about letting our thoughts and feelings lead us into despair?

Day 44

Read Psalm 44

There's a popular hymn which says: "Trust and obey, for there's no other way to be happy in Jesus, but to trust and obey." The truth in this song is that there is joy in a life of obedience. However, there may be times when we are trusting and obeying the Lord, yet problems come and rob us of joy. At such times, we may wonder: What is God doing in my life?

In Psalm 44, all God's people cry out to the Lord. The psalm can be divided into three parts. In verses 1 to 8, the Sons of Korah remember God's faithfulness in the past. He rescued them from Egypt and brought them into the promised land (v. 2). He alone gave them victory by His mighty power (vv. 3, 5–7). Why was He so kind to Israel? "For you loved them" (v. 3). He promised them that, as long as they remained faithful to His covenant, they could trust Him to keep on rescuing them from their enemies and blessing them (see Deuteronomy 28).

"But . . . you no longer go out with our armies" (Psalm 44:9). Now, God's people are confused. God had promised blessings as a reward for obedience. They have been faithful to His covenant, but He appears to have allowed their enemies to triumph over them (v. 10). What event in Israel's life is the psalm referring to? Perhaps when Assyria attacked Israel during the reign of godly Hezekiah (2 Kings 18–19), or when Moab and Ammon came against faithful Jehoshaphat (2 Chronicles 20). On both occasions, Israel was enjoying a time of spiritual renewal, but faced "a day of distress" (2 Kings 19:3).

In the final part of the psalm (Psalm 44:23–26), Israel asks God to wake up. Once, when Jesus' disciples were in a boat in the midst of a terrifying storm, they cried out to Jesus, who was sleeping: "Lord, save us!" (Matthew 8:25).

There will be times in this life when the ways of God will seem confusing to us. However, we know more than Israel about the power of God, and how He has demonstrated His love for us through the sacrifice of His Son (Romans 5:8). **We may not have all the answers, but we can trust a Father who "in all things . . . works for the good of those who love him"** (8:28).

ThinkThrough

Read Romans 8:36. In describing some of the sufferings we face, Paul quotes Psalm 44:22. How does Romans 8 give us a fuller answer to the questions posed by Psalm 44?

The foundation for Israel's hope in God is the story of how He saved them. How can we, as individual Christians and as a church, ensure that we remember, "what you did . . . in days long ago (Psalm 44:1)?

Day 45

Read Psalm 45

My wedding day was among the happiest of my life. I was finally united with my beautiful bride. All around me were dear family and friends. Psalm 45 is a glorious song celebrating the wedding of God's anointed king to his beautiful bride.

The climax of the Bible is a picture of the wedding feast of the Lamb (Revelation 19:6–9). From the outset we need to read this psalm of the wedding of God's king through the lens of its fulfilment in the Lord Jesus. He is the perfect king and the bride is His church, beautifully adorned for her husband (Ephesians 5:25–33; Revelation 21:2).

The king that Psalm 45 praises is quite possibly Solomon. The psalm begins by celebrating the grace and power of the king, who is clothed with splendour and majesty (v. 3). He is a champion of truth, humility, and justice (v. 4). His kingdom is "for ever and ever" (v. 6). These verses must point forward to another, different kind of king, because the rule of the house of David ended with Zedekiah and the fall of Jerusalem in 586 BC. Hebrews 1:8–9 quotes Psalm 45:6–7 to demonstrate the superiority of Jesus over all created things. The writer of Hebrews understood that while the psalm, in its original context, was referring to the Lord's commitment to David and his descendants, it found its true fulfilment in Jesus the eternal king.

In Psalm 45:10 the focus shifts to the bride. She is told to "forget your people". She must now leave her past behind her and be totally devoted to her husband and king (vv. 10–11). This same call is given to all who follow Jesus. Jesus told His disciples to leave their nets and families, and to follow Him (Mark 1:16–20).

The psalm also rejoices in the beauty of the bride. She joyfully gives herself to the king, who is now her lord (Psalm 45:11). After they are married she will bear the king sons, and these sons "will take the place of your fathers" (v. 16), and so the rule of the king will be extended throughout the world.

The church is the bride of Christ. **Like a young couple eagerly waiting for their wedding day, we look forward to the time when we will finally and eternally be with our King.** Psalm 45 is a glorious celebration of that day.

ThinkThrough

Read Psalm 45 again. In what other ways does this psalm point forward to the life and ministry of the Lord Jesus?

What is it about weddings that make this earthly celebration such a powerful picture of a heavenly reality?

Day 46

Read Psalm 46

Fear is one of the most common of all human emotions. We fear outward threats like war and disaster. We have inner fears like the prospect of failure. One of the tragic marks of life in a world which has rejected God is that we live with fear. The first words Adam said to God after he sinned were: "I heard you in the garden, and I was afraid" (Genesis 3:10). Fear now entered our world.

Psalm 46 brings comfort to a city gripped by fear. The first of the three stanzas (vv. 1–3) begins with a statement of faith that is the heading for all that follows: "God is our refuge and strength" (v. 1). **Our troubles change but God remains the same.** The imagery is terrifying: the crisis is like the quaking of the mountains, which are shaking so powerfully that they are tossed into the sea (vv. 2–3). But our comfort is that we are safe and secure in the Lord (v. 1).

In verses 4–7, the mood changes. Imagine Psalm 46 as a symphony. The first stanza is loud with crashing drums and blaring trumpets. Then, in the second stanza there is an abrupt change. Suddenly all is quiet, like the gentle plucking of harps. Instead of a raging river there is a peaceful, flowing river (v. 4). There is actually no river running through Jerusalem; it is poetry—a picture of peace and water which brings life. The Lord is watching over His people and protecting them. While around them the nations rage against them, God's city is at peace, for the Lord is in its midst (v. 5).

The triumphant final stanza (vv. 8–10) sings of the future when our great God will make wars cease. Psalm 46:10 is a frequently misunderstood verse. When God calls out: "Be still, and know that I am God", He is not speaking in a gentle voice. He is not saying: "In your busyness find rest in me." No, God is loudly commanding all the nations caught up in wars and aggression: "Stop your fighting! I am God!"

The day will come when God will say to all the warring nations: "Enough! I will destroy the weapons of your warfare." Then He will remove forever all those things that cause us fear. Hallelujah! Come, Lord Jesus!

ThinkThrough

What are the things in life that cause you to fear? What comfort does Psalm 46 bring?

Psalm 46 speaks of God protecting His people when disaster comes. How do we reconcile this with other psalms lamenting about how God has not protected them (e.g. Psalm 44)?

Day 47

Read Psalm 47

The main Christian celebrations are Christmas and Easter, when we remember three great events of the life of the Lord Jesus: His birth, His death, and His resurrection. By comparison, the church rarely speaks of Jesus' ascension. Yet our Lord's ascension to God's right hand, from where He rules the nations, is an event of global and eternal importance. Psalm 47 celebrates the ascension of the Great King, the Lord God.

Psalm 47 continues the triumphant theme of Psalm 46, in which we read of God silencing the raging of the nations. Here, He is praised because He has "subdued nations under us" (47:3). Presumably, this song was composed after a great victory. One can easily imagine Israel singing this song as David brought the ark of the covenant into Jerusalem, having defeated his enemies (2 Samuel 6). Psalm 47 is like a sandwich. The calls to praise God are the bread (vv. 1–4; 6–9), and the ascension of God is the meat (v. 5).

The psalm invites the nations to "shout to God with cries of joy" (v. 1). Whenever an ancient songwriter wanted to emphasise a truth, he would use repetition. So, five times in just nine verses, the Sons of Korah call on all people to sing praises to the Lord. It is surprising that even the subdued nations are called upon to praise God. Surely their defeat is more a cause for fear than joy? However, they can rejoice because as the God of Abraham (v. 9), He had promised that through Abraham all the nations of the earth would be blessed (Genesis 12:2–3). From His exalted throne, God will pour blessings on the nations.

At the centre of Psalm 47, we read that God has ascended to His throne (v. 5). Today, the rule of God and His Son is hidden from most people. **But one day, the curtain will be pulled back and then all will see that He reigns over the nations and is greatly exalted** (vv. 8–9). Whether we are troubled by disturbing events in our world or our personal struggles, today the five-fold call of Psalm 47 is to praise the God who "is seated on his holy throne" (v. 8).

ThinkThrough

Why do you think Christians do not give much attention to the ascension of Jesus? Why is this event so important to us?

Why do you think Psalm 47 chose to describe God's people as "the pride of Jacob, whom he loved" (v. 4)?

Day 48

Read Psalm 48

In the 1970s, a new wave of Christian music called "Scripture in Song" became popular; it was the result of an effort by a recording company to better incorporate Scripture into contemporary worship music. One of its earliest songs was based on Psalm 48, which I remember singing many times as a young Christian. However, at the time I didn't understand why we were singing a song in praise of Jerusalem. Why was I, a Christian, rejoicing in a city which was destroyed by the Babylonians and also the place where the Messiah was rejected and murdered?

Psalm 48 begins by placing the focus of worship where it should be: "Great is the LORD, and most worthy of praise" (v. 1). **While the psalm rejoices in Zion, the city's beauty and strength lies not in her strategic location, but in the fact that "God is in her citadels"** (v. 3). Essentially, this is a psalm in praise of God.

Mount Zion is a hill in Jerusalem that stands roughly 760 metres above sea level. Surrounded by mountainous terrain, Jerusalem was a difficult city to invade, as the long sieges by the armies of nations like Assyria and Babylon show. Verses 4 to 8 sing of the impregnability of Zion. However, it wasn't really the city itself which repulsed the invaders, sending them reeling in horror, but God in her midst: "You destroyed them . . ." (v. 7).

Verses 9 to 11 remind the singers of where the greatness of the city lies: it is where the people see and experience God's love, righteousness, and justice.

The psalm concludes with an invitation to "walk about Zion" (v. 12). When Nehemiah completed the rebuilding of the city's walls, he told two choirs to walk around them, in opposite directions, and "the sound of rejoicing in Jerusalem could be heard far away" (Nehemiah 12:31–43). Perhaps they sang Psalm 48!

Today, when we read and sing Psalm 48, our thoughts should turn to another Zion. As God's people, we can look forward to a more glorious Jerusalem. In Revelation 21:2–4, the church is portrayed as the holy city coming down from heaven. There is great joy because "God's dwelling-place is now among the people" (v. 3). Ancient Jerusalem symbolised God's people in God's place under God's rule. But that ancient city rebelled and was destroyed. Now, we look forward to the eternal city, the time when the Lord will dwell among us in perfect and unending love, righteousness, and justice.

ThinkThrough

Psalm 48:12–13 encourages us to behold the strength of Zion, and then proclaim this to the next generation. How do we apply these verses to the church today?

Why do you think Revelation 21:2–4 describes God's people as a city? What is it about a city that makes it an appropriate picture for God and His church?

Day 49

Read Psalm 49

The book of Hebrews gives a summary of life in saying: "People are destined to die once, and after that to face judgment" (Hebrews 9:27). Of course, there is much more to our time on earth than waiting for death and judgment, but this highlights the importance of giving serious thought to the fact—and implication—of these two great realities. Or, in the words of Psalm 49: "People, despite their wealth, do not endure" (v. 12).

To read Psalm 49 is to enter the world of the wisdom books like Proverbs and Ecclesiastes. The psalm is addressed to the rich who have placed false security in their wealth. It is true that, under the old covenant, one of the marks of God's blessing was material wealth. This has changed under the new covenant, where God's blessings are primarily spiritual. But it is also true that wealth was never a guarantee of membership in God's kingdom. Indeed, as we have seen in the psalms, God regularly used the term "the poor" to describe His people (e.g. 37:14).

Psalm 49 proclaims the path of salvation from death. We are told that a human life is so precious that all the money in the world cannot ransom it from the grave (vv. 7–9). What price, then, can be paid to ransom someone from death, and who can pay that price? The question posed by Psalm 49 is answered by the gospel. **God has redeemed us, not with perishable things such as silver and gold, "but with the precious blood of Christ"** (1 Peter 1:18–19).

Then the psalm brings a word of warning to those who trust in themselves, and an encouragement to the righteous. The rich are like sheep who follow their shepherd—Death—all the way to the grave (Psalm 49:14). However, those who trust in the Lord can confidently say: "God will redeem me from the realm of the dead, he will surely take me to himself" (v. 15).

Psalm 49 is one of the clearest proofs we have that believers under the old covenant believed that after death they would live and be with their Lord. We who have put our trust in Jesus have an even greater certainty, because of our "living hope through the resurrection of Jesus Christ from the dead" (1 Peter 1:3).

ThinkThrough

How can we be tempted to envy the rich? Why is it that having riches sometimes blinds people from seeing spiritual realities?

The Bible suggests that it is wise to remember the reality of death (see 1 Timothy 6:6–10). How can we remind others of this truth appropriately and sensitively?

Day 50

Read Psalm 50

At the Bible college where I once served as its principal, there were "staff performance reviews" at the end of each year. This is common in many organisations; such reviews provide an opportunity to commend and encourage those who have worked well, and to reprimand those whose work has been unsatisfactory.

Psalm 50 is a fitting conclusion to our journey through the first part of Psalms. The scene is like a courtroom. The Lord has summoned all heaven and earth to sit in the gallery and watch the proceedings (v. 1). The judge is God (v. 4), and He is terrifying. He is not sitting silently in His robes—in fact, tempest and fire rage around Him (v. 3). Before Him is Israel, the people He has set apart for himself (v. 5).

First, God speaks a general word to all His people (vv. 7–15). As part of the covenant, the people were required to make sacrifices (see Leviticus 1:1–6:7). While necessary, the sacrifices were always intended to be an outward expression of an inner spiritual reality. Like some of our Christian activities such as Holy Communion, the important thing was the state of the heart, not the outward action. The people had followed carefully the instructions for making sacrifices—but had forgotten to give to the Lord the better sacrifice of a thankful and trusting heart (Psalm 50:14).

God doesn't need our sacrifices, but we need Him. Above all, He wants us to depend on Him, to "call on me in the day of trouble" (v. 15).

In verses 16 to 22, God speaks directly to the wicked within Israel. He exposes their hypocrisy. They recite God's laws with their lips (v. 16), but then go on to break the commandments which forbid theft, adultery, and bearing false witness (vv. 18–20; see Exodus 20:14–16). They now stand condemned in God's courtroom. There is still time, though, to change. They need to "consider this" before judgment comes (Psalm 50:22).

Appropriately, the psalm—and this book—ends with a summary of what God desires of His people. He wants the sacrifice—not of a bull or sheep, but of a thankful heart. How much more can we today be thankful to our God who, as we saw in Psalm 49, has ransomed us by the gift of His Son! A thankful heart finds expression in a blameless life. God, our Judge, will not condemn us. Instead, we have His promise in Psalm 50:23: "I will show my salvation."

ThinkThrough

Can you think of Christian practices that can easily become religious rituals whose true meaning and purpose we have forgotten?

On two occasions God speaks of His delight in our giving thanks (Psalm 50:14, 23). As we conclude our journey through the first part of Psalms, spend some time offering your thanks and praises to God, our Redeemer, King, and Judge.

Journey Through

Proverbs

The book of Proverbs is much, much more than a poetic collection of pithy, common-sense sayings. Dig deep into the teachings of Solomon, Agur, Lemuel, and others, and you'll be surprised by what you can learn from these men of ancient wisdom. You'll discover why true wisdom begins with "the fear of the Lord", how a relationship of reverence and love for God will lead to true knowledge, and how contemporary and relevant the book of Proverbs continues to be for life today.

David Cook was Principal of the Sydney Missionary and Bible College for 26 years. He is an accomplished writer and has authored Bible commentaries, books on the Minor Prophets, and several Bible study guides.

Journey Through

Ruth

She was poor, widowed, and a member of a tribe whom Israel hated. Yet she chose to follow her mother-in-law home, and become a foreigner in a land she had never seen. It would lead to an unusual love story—a story that would end with Ruth becoming the ancestor of one of Israel's greatest rulers, and of its true King. What can we learn from the choices Ruth and others made? And what does it tell us about God's hand in their lives? Journey through the book of Ruth, and discover how we can be part of God's story as He leads us to accomplish His divine plan.

Sim Kay Tee is a longtime pastor and preacher, and serves at Our Daily Bread Ministries as a Bible teacher, writer, and theological reviewer. A regular contributor to *Our Daily Bread*, Kay Tee is deeply passionate about God's Word and teaching it to His people. He is the proud parent of three daughters and one granddaughter.

Journey Through

Esther

The story of how a young woman conquers challenging circumstances to save her people is a dramatic one. It is a tale of courage and self-sacrifice. But where is God in the story? And what can we learn from Esther, the reluctant heroine who rises to the occasion when she realises she has been placed "for such a time as this"? Dig into the book of Esther with Peter Lau and discover how you can live as God's delivered people in a hostile world.

Peter Lau has been lecturing at Seminari Theoloji Malaysia since 2010. He is a trained medical doctor, and also holds a PhD in Old Testament. He has published on Ruth, Ezekiel, and Psalms. Peter is married to Kathryn and they have three children.

Journey Through

Judges

The book of Judges describes a low point in the history of God's people. It tells of a time of moral and spiritual anarchy, when everyone ignored God's life-giving laws and did what they thought was right in their own eyes. It is a story of disobedience and defeat. Yet the book also contains glimpses of the Israelites' capacity for greatness—when they chose to trust and depend on God. Discover God's great principles of life, and find out how we can lead powerful, productive lives in a society that is increasingly hostile to our faith.

Gary Inrig is a graduate of the University of British Columbia and Dallas Theological Seminary. An established Bible teacher and former pastor, he has authored several books, including *True North, The Parables, Forgiveness,* and *Whole Marriages in a Broken World.*

For information on our resources, visit **ourdailybread.org**. Alternatively, please contact the office nearest you from the list below, or go to **ourdailybread.org/locations** for the complete list of offices.

BELARUS
Our Daily Bread Ministries
PO Box 82, Minsk, Belarus 220107
belarus@odb.org • (375-17) 2854657; (375-29) 9168799

GERMANY
Our Daily Bread Ministries e.V.
Schulstraße 42, 79540 Lörrach
deutsch@odb.org • +49 (0) 7621 9511135

IRELAND
Our Daily Bread Ministries
64 Baggot Street Lower, Dublin 2, D02 XC62
ireland@odb.org • +353 (0) 1676 7315

RUSSIA
MISSION Our Daily Bread
PO Box "Our Daily Bread",
str.Vokzalnaya 2, Smolensk, Russia 214961
russia@odb.org • 8(4812)660849; +7(951)7028049

UKRAINE
Christian Mission Our Daily Bread
PO Box 533, Kiev, Ukraine 01004
ukraine@odb.org • +380964407374; +380632112446

UNITED KINGDOM (Europe Regional Office)
Our Daily Bread Ministries
PO Box 1, Millhead, Carnforth, LA5 9ES
europe@odb.org • +44 (0)15395 64149

ourdailybread.org

JourneyThrough™
Matthew
62 Daily Insights from God's Word by Mike Raiter
JourneyThrough™
Mark
Daily Insights from God's Word by Robert M. Solomon
JourneyThrough™
Luke
62 Daily Insights from God's Word by Mike Raiter
JourneyThrough™
John
50 Daily Insights from God's Word by David Cook

Sign up to *Journey Through*

We would love to support you with the *Journey Through* series! Please be aware we can only provide one copy of each future *Journey Through* book per reader (previous books from the series are available to purchase).

If you know of other people who would be interested in this series, we can send you introductory *Journey Through* booklets to pass onto them (which include details on how they can easily sign up for the books themselves).

- ☐ **I would like to regularly receive the *Journey Through* series**
- ☐ **Please send me ____ copies of the *Journey Through* introductory booklet**

Just complete and return this sign up form to us at:

Our Daily Bread Ministries,
PO Box 1, Millhead,
Carnforth, LA5 9ES,
United Kingdom

Here at Our Daily Bread Ministries we take your privacy seriously. We will only use this personal information to manage your account, and regularly provide you with *Journey Through* series books and offers of other resources, three ministry update letters each year, and occasional additional mailings with news that's relevant to you. We will also send you ministry updates and details of Discovery House products by email if you agree to this. In order to do this we share your details with our UK-based mailing house and Our Daily Bread Ministries in the US. We do not sell or share personal information with anyone for marketing purposes.

Please do not complete and sign this form for anyone but yourself. You do not need to complete this form if you already receive regular copies of *Journey Through* from us.

Full Name (Mr/Mrs/Miss/Ms): ______________________________

Address: ______________________________

____

Postcode: ______________________ Tel: ______________________

Email: ______________________________

☐ I would like to receive email updates and details of Our Daily Bread Publishing products.

Signature: ______________________________

All our resources, including *Journey Through*, are available without cost. Many people, making even the smallest of donations, enable Our Daily Bread Ministries to reach others with the life-changing wisdom of the Bible. We are not funded or endowed by any group or denomination.